WE HEARD SHOOTING. We didn't just hear it—we felt it. *Shutt! Shutt!* The noise streaked past us. Helmut and I plodded behind the wagon, fearing to look to the side. We bowed our heads and prayed as we walked.

I had a queasy feeling in my stomach. A sense of foreboding settled on me. Fearful questions sped through my mind. *Will I ever see my parents again? How can my mother escape, crippled as she is? Who will pray for me now that we are in danger?* With tears streaming down my cheeks, I asked God to take care of my mother and Ruth.

This is my last trip, I thought. *My very last trip.*

Blessings —

Irma Stoll

Psalm 37:4.5

The Sparrow's Song

IRMA STOLL
with
CATHARINE BRANDT

Greenlawn Press

Scripture verses are taken from the *King James Version (KJV)* and *The Living Bible (TLB)* unless otherwise noted.

ISBN 0-937779-19-9

Library of Congress Catalog Card Number 83-51672

© 1984 by Irma Stoll. All rights reserved. Except for brief quotations in critical articles and reviews, no part of this book may be reproduced in any manner without prior written permission from the publisher. Write to:
Greenlawn Press
107 S. Greenlawn
South Bend, IN 46617

Originally published by Tyndale House Publishers, Inc.

Printed in the United States of America

To
my two sons,
Sieghard and Hans,
who have never known
the early life
of their mother

CONTENTS

1. "Nothing to Worry About" 15
2. Early Days in East Prussia 25
3. The Russians Invade Germany 31
4. "Frau, komm" 37
5. Captured 45
6. The March to Poland 53
7. Starving in a Cattle Car 61
8. Arriving in Siberia 69
9. Slave Labor 75
10. A Glimpse of Russian Life 83
11. The Train on the Other Track 95
12. Search for Family 105
13. Crossing Over 111
14. Rebuilding Life 117

   EPILOGUE
   Greater Dimensions 127

ACKNOWLEDGMENTS

I am forever grateful to my parents for their love and Christian example. Without that commitment to me, I would never have survived the rigors of slave labor, and to this day their lives have blessed me.

The writing of this book has been in the back of my mind for a long time. And it took much prayer to restore the memory of years gone by.

My love and appreciation are also given to my husband, John, whose encouragement motivated me to write this book. Then I wish to thank my many friends who wanted to read my life story.

Finally I want to thank my friend Catharine Brandt for her willingness and ability to put this story into writing.

INTRODUCTION

Since the beginning of time God has put great emphasis on the family. He has given parents a mandate to instruct their children in the way they should go: "And you must think constantly about these commandments I am giving you today. You must teach them to your children and talk about them when you are at home or out for a walk; at bedtime and the first thing in the morning" (Deut. 6:6, 7, TLB).

I have often thanked God for allowing me to be born into a Christian family. My parents taught their five children to love and honor God. They held family devotions, and were concerned about the spiritual health of us children. My father was an elder, a lay minister; and my mother, in spite of great physical pain, had a song in her heart and on her lips. One of my earliest recollections is of my mother singing favorite hymns: "What a Friend We Have in Jesus," and "It Is Well with My Soul."

The youngest of five, I can't remember a time when I didn't love Jesus and consider him my Friend. Although I did not know fully that it was "well with my soul," I felt at peace with the world.

As a child I had no way of knowing what persecution lay ahead for us as German citizens. In my sheltered home my young mind couldn't imagine the torture, deprivation, and degradation I would endure.

Today no one knows what lies ahead for America's youth nor what persecution any of us may endure. Already many hesitate to walk city streets at night for fear of violence. The hardships of strikes and unemployment loom. Many Americans know what it means to be without food, fuel, warm clothing, and money.

How will our children withstand such difficulties? The best preparation is faith in the heavenly Father. How thankful I am for parents who taught me spiritual truths and trust in God. All through my ordeal I knew my parents prayed for me, and I trusted God to protect and guide me.

And he did! Here is my story.

*Not one
sparrow . . . can fall to
the ground without
your Father knowing it.*

Matthew 10:29
The Living Bible

ONE
"Nothing to Worry About"

All week long the radio screamed, "Everything is fine. Nothing to worry about. We will win the war." We had no television, and telephone communication had ceased.

Yet my sister Edeltraut and I couldn't help but worry. Our father, two brothers, and Edeltraut's husband had been conscripted into Hitler's army. We grew uneasy as we watched German soliders move closer and closer.

At first, from my sister's farmhouse in East Prussia, not far from Mohrungen in what is now Poland, we saw only an occasional soldier marching past. But now many kept moving in around us. In spite of the messages the radio blared, we sensed the general uneasiness. Our world as we knew it was ready to explode.

Early in 1945, when I was fifteen, I had

been designated to make my *pflichtjahr* (a year of compulsory service in a home with small children). Hitler encouraged large families and provided young girls to help mothers. I was fortunate that my assignment was to my sister's farm.

Edeltraut, mother of three small children, was expecting another. Her aged mother-in-law lived with her. Max, a captured Ukrainian who took care of the livestock and outside chores, was good to the children and a help to my sister in the absence of her husband.

One Sunday morning my sister said, "Irma, I don't know whether we should go to church today." Edeltraut did not make decisions lightly. I thought she was numbed by the responsibilities thrust upon her. The war had been going on for several years. She was never quite sure what to do. I was more apt to plunge in.

"Why don't we go?" I asked. "We may hear important news."

"Yes, we might." Then Edeltraut told Max to hitch up the horses. I began dressing the children in warm clothing. Edeltraut's mother-in-law whimpered that she didn't want to move away from the fire. I told her we were going to church, and she seemed satisfied. When we were ready, Max lifted the children onto the sled, the rest of us climbed on, and my sister drove off.

A fresh snow covered the ground that Sunday in 1945. Our sleigh bells jingled, and we sat snug in a lamb's-wool lap robe. *Like a painting of a snow scene,* I thought. But no peaceful winter scene lay ahead of us. When we reached the meetinghouse, we saw only a few sleds. Deciding the snow must have kept people home, we tossed the lap robe aside and walked in. Several friends sat quietly praying and reading their Bibles.

"Why did you waste time coming?" they asked. "Haven't you heard everyone is fleeing as fast as possible? The Russians are marching in. It's not safe to stay here."

My sister stared in disbelief. I shivered with fear. We had heard shocking tales of the enemy, tales of torture and rape, vandalism and shooting. All we could think of now was: *Get out and get out fast!* Lugging the children and their grandmother with us, we ran outside, jumped on the sled, and started back to the farm.

"We have to take all the food and blankets we can," Edeltraut said. After a moment, she added, "Let's go to Tante Hedwig's first. She wasn't in church, and we should warn her." Edeltraut gave the horses' reins a flick, and we sped down the road toward our aunt's house. No spiral of smoke rose from the chimney as we drove up the lane. We knocked, opened the door, and called, "Anyone home?" No answer told us Tante Hedwig and her family had already fled, leaving her house with its beautiful furnishings. We scurried back to the sled and headed for Edeltraut's farm.

When we reached home, Edeltraut explained the situation to Max. We had picked up a few Russian words from him, and he had learned some German ones. Max understood and at once unhitched the horses from the sled, fed them, and moved them over to the wagon.

"Wagon better than sled," he told us. "Snow melts."

I tried to make the children's grandmother understand we had to flee, but like a child she needed directions repeated. Her constant complaining and crying upset the children. "Here, Grandma," I said to her as I sliced bread and poured warm milk, "eat something. We're going on a trip."

Edeltraut collected canned beef and pork chops and whatever else she thought we could use from her well-stocked pantry. We hastily packed the food into empty milk cans that would serve as coolers, while Max filled one can with milk.

All the while Edeltraut kept repeating, "I don't know where we should go. What will happen to us?" A firm knock on the door made us both tremble with fear. Until we opened it.

There stood our brother Helmut leaning on a cane. "Why are you still here?" he demanded. "Haven't you heard the Russians are advancing? Get out as quick as you can." He began loading food and bedding into the wagon. My sister perked up. His coming was just what she needed—someone to take charge.

"And why are you here, Helmut?" she asked.

He told us that though wounded, he had left the hospital. "I was trying to get up to Palmnicken [a town on the Baltic seacoast] to help my family, but all the trains are bombed out, and this is as far as I can go. There's no communication so I thought I'd check on you girls."

As I fed the children and Grandma, I tried to overcome my own fear. I was alarmed not only for our safety, but also for my parents'. My father and my sister Ruth's husband were in the army. My mother and Ruth were left home alone. What would happen to them if they had to flee? My mother, crippled by arthritis, couldn't walk very far, and Ruth was expecting her first child soon.

My thoughts made me edgy, and I spanked the oldest boy for teasing his sister. I felt we were going around in circles. Like a nightmare, everything we did appeared unreal, slowed down. Nothing was turning out right.

Helmut urged us to hurry, but Edeltraut found one more necessity after the other to take. In a time of disaster people forget about heirloom silver and wedding pictures, thinking instead of food and pans, warm clothing and blankets. After dressing the children and Grandma in coats and caps, I put on the fur jacket my mother had given me the last time she had visited us. Then I picked up the red mittens she had knit for me.

Max lifted the children and Grandma into the wagon and tucked blankets around them. The milk cans of food hung on the sides of the wagon.

"Why are we going on this trip?" cried the old lady. I had already explained to her half a dozen times that it wasn't safe to stay, but she couldn't remember.

Helmut, Max, and I walked alongside the wagon and horses to lighten the load. Helmut and I talked about our mother and sister Ruth and how it was impossible to visit them now. The German army was everywhere. If people started one way, the soldiers turned them back into the flow of traffic. I think the soldiers realized it was too late to do anything.

As we took off, we could hear what sounded like thunder in the distance. "It's not thunder," Helmut told us. "It's guns. Armored tanks." Nearing the road to town, we encountered great confusion. We had no choice but to join others with packed wagons and sleds as well as people on foot carrying what possessions they could.

Night was falling fast, but we kept going until we reached a wooded area near a small town. Among the trees stood a big farmhouse and nearby a small house where the help usually lived. Several wagons and horses stood there. Edeltraut's children began to cry and Grandma started to complain. With darkness upon us we had to sleep someplace. We hoped that we, too, could find shelter for the night. Helmut directed the horses to turn aside.

Knocking on the door, my sister asked if we could stay the night. The room was crowded with people, but nobody appeared to be in charge. I sensed they, too, were frightened and found comfort being together.

"Always room for one more," someone said with a laugh. Max left to take care of the horses, and we filed into the crowded little room.

When Max came back, he took us aside. "The Russians are moving closer," he told us quietly. "I'm going to run for it. If they find me, it will be hard on all of us." My sister wrapped some food for him. He left sometime in the night, and we never saw him again. (In the days since that time I have often thought of Max, a captured enemy soldier whom God used to help my sister in a time of trouble.)

We talked to a neighbor woman whose daughter Ingrid was about my age. Ingrid and I whispered, and she told me that her father had stayed home to care for the cattle. (Later when we drove past their farm we saw that he had been shot to death, and the animals turned loose.) We found comfort being close to each other at such a dangerous time, even if we did bump into one another. Finally we made beds on the floor and slept as best we could.

Early in the morning we peeked out the window. German soldiers had disappeared, and Russian ones had taken their place. A woman rushed in, frightened and upset. "The Russians are coming here," she cried. "Quick, you girls hide." All of us had heard enough war stories to know the Russians looked for two things—watches and young girls.

"Run into that small room and shut the door," one old man told us. "We'll hang coats over it and move the furniture in front of the door." Ingrid, Edeltraut, and I ran into the little room.

Another woman pointed to Helmut. "He should hide, too," she said. "They'll wonder why he's here and not in the army and maybe kill us all." Helmut followed us. We stood silent and frozen with fear in the little room as the others hung coats and moved furniture in front of the door.

Suddenly the outside door banged open, and we heard heavy stomping and gruff voices. "Any German soldiers hiding here?" they asked. "Any young girls?" My throat felt dry, the palms of my hands wet. "Give us your watches!"

Although some of the people understood, they pretended not to. The enemy stalked around until suddenly we heard the furniture being shoved aside and coats being pulled away. Finally the door separating us was yanked open.

Facing us stood two soldiers with machine guns pointed at us. "Stick up your hands," they ordered, showing us what they meant. Trembling, we raised our arms while they searched for watches and valuables. When they saw Helmut's wedding ring, they tried to pull it off, but his swollen fingers held it fast. Helmut, not wanting to give up his ring, shrank back. I prayed he would give it to them. I was afraid they would shoot him if he didn't. Finally, wrenching Helmut's finger, a soldier pulled the ring off. Then they turned and stomped out of the room without harming us.

But we knew they would return. It was not safe for us to remain. My sister and Helmut talked it over and decided to go back to her farm. "It couldn't be worse," Edeltraut said. Ingrid and her mother joined us.

On the way to Edeltraut's farm we heard shooting from the left and the right. We didn't just hear it—we felt it. *Shutt! Shutt!* The noise streaked past us. Helmut and I plodded behind the wagon, fearing to look to the side. We bowed our heads and prayed as we walked.

I had a queasy feeling in the pit of my stomach. A sense of foreboding settled on me. Fearful questions sped through my mind. *Will I ever see my parents again? How can my mother escape, crippled as she is? Who will pray for me now that we are in danger?* With tears streaming down my cheeks, I asked God to take care of my mother and Ruth. *This is my last trip,* I thought. *My very last trip.*

TWO
Early Days in East Prussia

During the late 1930s my parents knew more than they talked about. Only a child, I, nevertheless, sensed their apprehension. On the radio we heard pep talks of how wonderful Germany was and of how Hitler would build our country into the greatest nation in the world. But my father knew better. His work as a builder took him from place to place in East Prussia, and he could see that our country was on the brink of collapse.

"Germany can't go on like this," he told my mother. "We are headed for disaster. The Lord will not let injustice go on too long."

My parents rejected Hitler's demands whenever possible. They were against what he imposed on the German people even though they didn't dare openly oppose him. My father said he had to take care of his invalid wife, so he didn't join the Nazi *Partei* (Party). My parents found excuses to keep us away from the Hitler youth groups as much as possible. And they spent time teaching us spiritual truths and reading the Bible aloud.

As the youngest of five children, I knew a warm, well-loved feeling. I had been born in Thomareinen, Krs. Osterode, a beautiful region of lakes and forests in East Prussia. My father had bought a house with land there and had built a water mill on the river that ran through our property. At times, especially before thunderstorms, large bass, walleye, and northern pike would swim into the mill wheel and stop it. My brothers would then pull the fish out and fill a barrel with them. My mother knew how to prepare fish in many ways.

My brothers and sisters and I often picked berries and mushrooms near our home. We raised our own livestock, chickens, and bees for honey. My mother made butter and cheese and baked bread every week. She used to rinse our wash in the clear, cold stream water, even in winter when she had to chop a hole in the ice. It was quicker than carrying buckets of water from the pump.

Our home there was always open to visitors. Sometimes we had as many as twenty people around the dinner table. My father built a large room onto our house for community worship services and Bible study—he did most of the teaching and preaching.

Because of the dishonesty of the former owner of our home, my father lost all he had put into the property, and we had to move. The story of how my parents had risen above their misfortunes became part of our family history. My father had taken the man at his word, but had learned that not everyone can be trusted.

My parents were hardworking, and taught us children to work hard, too. We were not to let the dishonesty of others or inflation or war get us down. We were to trust God no matter what.

The evening was the best time of the day at our house. My father was jolly and outgoing, and his voice boomed out. We had fun and laughed a lot. I enjoyed sitting with my parents by the fire in the early evening hours when my father would tell stories about World War I or play games with me.

When my mother was only fifty, she was stricken with rheumatoid arthritis and became badly crippled. Ruth and I had to do most of the housework while my mother spent several months in the hospital.

One day after school as I visited her, I looked out the back window. A flock of chickens the hospital raised for food was making a big disturbance. A hospital attendant had set down a bowl of steaming hot scraps for the chickens. Just then a group of Russian prisoners marched by with a German guard. One Russian, gaunt and haggard, walked away from the others. Leaning over the bowl of chicken scraps, he scooped a handful and crammed it into his mouth. The

German guard shouted and swore at the prisoner, pushing him back into line.

I turned to my mother and said, "Mama, if someone is hungry enough to eat scraps set out for the chickens, why not give it to him?"

"Yes," my mother replied. "It will all come back to us someday. It is not right. The Lord will not leave such acts unpunished."

The incident left a deep impression on me. I had never seen anyone so heartless.

As time went on, my brothers were conscripted into the service. When Hitler's officers converted the churches into soldiers' barracks, my father and others at our church looked for a substitute.

"He closed the churches," my father said, "but he can't close the services." They found an empty room on the second floor of a nearby building and rented it, and we met there every Sunday.

When I was about fifteen, Deacon Kuhn, an elderly man who was almost blind and a good friend of the family, sat at our dinner table. We thanked God for the food, never doubting that God was the Provider in our lives. Then my father and Deacon Kuhn began talking seriously about the war and shortages. I listened with only one ear because I wanted to clear away the dishes and go out with my friends.

"Irma," said Deacon Kuhn, "you are pretty like your mother, the same blue eyes, the same hair like gold."

I could feel my face redden at such personal remarks. I flipped my braids over my shoulders and glanced at my mother's gray hair pulled back in a knot. *Was her hair really like mine when she was young?* I wondered. She smiled at me across the table.

Then Deacon Kuhn talked more personally to me. "Irma, don't you think it is time for you to be baptized?"

I had grown up in an old-tradition Baptist family, and my parents thought I was ready to be baptized and to join the church. In our church, baptism meant total commitment to Jesus Christ. Under the Nazi regime it was not easy to be a Christian. In my class at school I knew of just two who were Christians. The rest of the class pointed their fingers at us and made fun of us. It took a strong person to be an out-and-out Christian, and I was not ready.

At church others told of great experiences they had had after coming to Christ. "God saved me from certain death," one man said. "God healed my back," said another. "He answered my prayer for money for a good education," related one woman.

In my heart I knew I had no such experience to talk about. I didn't feel ready to commit my whole life to Jesus Christ. What experience had I had? None. I was just the youngest daughter of Hermann and Marie Dreipelcher. My religion was really my parents'. Because of their teaching I couldn't remember a time when I hadn't loved God and tried to obey him. Still I wanted an experience of my own, one that would show me God's power, one I could tell others about. I looked down at my plate.

Deacon Kuhn peered at me through kind, old eyes. "Jesus is standing at the door of your heart. Won't you open and let him in?" Then he prayed that I would come to a decision soon. At the time I was not aware of what lay ahead for Germany, but I'm certain my parents had an inkling. They were concerned about the spiritual health of their children.

"I would like to wait," I said softly.

Deacon Kuhn sat back in his chair. My mother sighed. In the silence I heard the kitchen clock ticking.

By 1944 a heavy cloud of anxiety hung over us. My parents knew the war was not going well for Germany. My two brothers and our minister had been conscripted into Hitler's army. In the minister's absence, my father, who was an elder and lay pastor, preached and prayed and held us together through those dark and questioning days.

Soon my father, too, was drafted into the service, leaving my mother, my sister Ruth, and me alone. Then I left to serve my *pflichtjahr* at Edeltraut's farm. That had been weeks ago.

All these recollections flashed through my mind as I trudged with Helmut behind the wagon. We were on the way back to Edeltraut's farm.

THREE
The Russians Invade Germany

Snow had fallen all night making the roads slushy. Helmut, Ingrid, and I trudged behind the wagon, our shoes soaking wet. The wagon wheels flung chunks of dirt and snow at us, spattering my blue skirt. The horses snorted and strained to pull the heavy wagon. Helmut climbed on and threw off two large boxes to lighten the load.

Edeltraut had her hands full driving the horses, so the neighbor lady who was riding with us tried to keep the children happy. Grandma cried in her high-pitched voice, "We never should have left home." Many wagons choked the narrow road, making it seemingly impossible for us to turn back and head for Edeltraut's farm. We rode in circles for a day or two trying to find a way back.

As we approached a small town near Edeltraut's farm, a horrible stench greeted us. Helmut grunted. "Dead soldiers," he said, turning his face straight ahead.

The town had been badly shelled. Germans lay lifeless along the ditches and across the road. I was revulsed when I unsuspectingly stepped on frozen arms and legs partly buried in the mud and snow. Caps and boots and mittens dotted the road.

As guns kept firing past us, I prayed that God would protect me through this horrible experience of war. I wondered what would happen to my father fighting somewhere and to my mother who would never be able to walk as we were doing.

As we tramped through the small town, practically destroyed by bombs and fire, Russians lined both sides of the street. They wore long khaki-colored coats and carried guns. Many were Mongolians. Unshaven and dirty they reached over and grabbed things from our wagon. After one quick glance at them I kept my eyes on the road, trying desperately not to step on the dead soldiers. As one soldier leaned toward me, I shrank back. He indicated he wanted my mittens, the warm red ones my mother had knitted.

"Hand them over," Helmut growled. I pulled off the mittens and handed them to the soldier. Another soldier began unfastening my fur jacket. Hurriedly I slipped out of it. *Anything,* I thought, *if that's all they want.* It was too cold for me to go without a jacket; so as we plodded along behind the wagon, I stooped beside the road to pick up a tattered coat, a mitten, and a glove. Briefly I wondered who had worn them before.

I was proud of Edeltraut driving the horses steadily on in spite of the shouts and calls of the soldiers along the road. What courage she had. From time to time Helmut called out directions to her, urging the horses on since dusk was falling fast. At last we left the other wagons and turned off the main road to the farm. The horses struggled up the rutted road. The children fussed for food. I wasn't hungry but I knew we had to eat for strength. Only God knew what lay in store for us.

Atop the barn was a ragged stork's nest outlined against the sky. When we reached Edeltraut's house, we roused the children and their grandmother. Helmut tugged open the door. Even in the twilight we could see something was wrong.

"Oh! Oh!" Edeltraut wailed as she stumbled against an overturned chair. "Stay where you are till I find candles." The bombs, of course, had knocked out the electricity.

Lighted candles in hand, we couldn't believe our eyes. The comfortable old house that Edeltraut had kept homey and clean was in a shambles. Vandals had torn curtains from the windows, had overturned the china cupboard, had thrown dishes to the floor, and dresser drawers had been dumped out. Slowly we walked from room to room. Everywhere vandalism sneered at us. I thought of the stork's nest, which Germans considered a good omen. But what was good about all this?

"Look at all the beds," I said. Beds without mattresses—just springs—stood in every room of the house, including the attic and even the kitchen. "Where did they come from?" I asked.

"They probably used the house as a barracks," Helmut said. He and I set the china cupboard upright, but I couldn't find a whole plate or cup to put in it.

"Did they have to break everything?" Edeltraut asked in despair. She stooped to pick up a picture which had been pulled from the wall, its glass shattered.

The children's grandmother began to cry. "We should have stayed home," she whimpered.

Edeltraut tried to comfort her. "It's all right, Mom. We'll fix things up quickly." To Helmut and me, Edeltraut whispered, "We are home, but what good is it? It was a mistake to come, but we have to eat and sleep. Then we can get cleaned up in the morning and go on." Getting cleaned up was important to my sister, but I just wanted to get away.

Helmut built a fire in the cook stove, and the neighbor lady and her daughter Ingrid helped prepare the food. Edeltraut picked up a broken plate. "It was an heirloom," she said sadly.

I wanted to say, "Never mind all that. We

have more important things to think about."
But I felt sorry for Edeltraut, eight months
pregnant as she was. How tired she must
have felt and how frightened, too. So I kept
quiet and opened a can of meat for our
supper.

After I fed the baby warm milk, I picked up
the next oldest boy, gave him a hug, and
tickled him to chase away his tears. While we
were eating, we heard a commotion outside.
Several Russian soldiers rode up on horses.
Of course the soldiers had spied the smoke
from our fire so they knew it was not a
"dead" house.

"Those are our horses," whispered Ingrid's
mother. "I recognize them. And ridden by
Mongolians!" she added.

They flung open the door and pushed in
with lanterns and flashlights. Dirty and
unshaven, noisy and brutish looking, the Russians helped themselves to meat and bread.
The leader stood in front of Helmut and
demanded, "What are you doing here?"
Although we understood some of his words,
we pretended we didn't know what he was
talking about.

"Komm," the soldiers said to Helmut,
pointing their guns at him. "For questions.
You can come back in a few days." As they
started to push Helmut out the door, he
grabbed his jacket and cane and said goodbye to us. From the open door we watched him
limping along in front of the Russian soldiers,
taking with him the confidence we had in an

older brother's strength and directions.

"We'll never see him again," cried my sister. "Who will tell us what to do?"

"We'll just have to figure out things for ourselves," I said more bravely than I felt. "Maybe we can sleep tonight and move on tomorrow. We can follow the other wagons and see where they go."

I picked up the broom and swept aside the broken dishes and all the mess, clearing a place where we could lie down for the night. We brought in blankets from the wagon and huddled together.

The last thing the children's grandmother said was "We never should have left home." I felt sorry for her, so old and confused and frightened. I, too, was frightened for the unknown tomorrow and wished that Helmut was still with us. I worried about him and wondered what had happened to him. Terrifying thoughts came to mind, and I cried myself to sleep.

FOUR
"*Frau,* komm"

With a start I woke up, then froze with fear.
In the stillness of the night I heard the sound
of horses and heavy boots pounding up the
steps. *The soldiers,* I thought. When they
opened the door, I could see it was still dark
outside. Because of the cold we had covered
our heads with blankets. I scrunched down
inside mine to hide my face. We had heard
tales of how the Russians looked for plump
young girls.

Flashlights shone into our faces and
around the room. A soldier yanked my
blanket aside and stared down at me. Ingrid
was tall and skinny and not very pretty,
which protected her from the soldiers this
time.

"Frau, *komm,*" the soldier said, gun held to
my head. I recalled unbelievable horror
stories I had heard at school about girls

being raped by the enemy and about what happened when they resisted. I wanted to scream, but I was too scared to cry out. I was only fifteen and nothing in my sheltered life had prepared me for what lay ahead.

The soldier jerked me upright and there was nothing to do but go. I prayed the children and Grandma would not wake up and cry out, for then we would probably all be shot.

They dragged me up to the attic, forced me to lie on one of the beds that had no mattress—only springs—and raped me. This was the most traumatic experience in all my fifteen years. I was almost numb with shock.

A soldier with a bayonet stood beside the bed. Downstairs I had thought only three or four soldiers had stomped inside, but now they stood in line at the door, and there must have been a dozen or more. I was terrified by their faces, for I had never seen Mongolians until the Russians had taken over. Also they were dirty and smelly as though they had come from the front line. It was a nightmare. I kept thinking, *This is not real. God, why are you allowing this to happen?*

Finally the soldiers shoved me out of the room, and I stumbled downstairs. I felt the soldiers at my back, clumping down after me, and I thought that at any moment they would shoot.

When they left the house, I crawled under the blanket with my sister. I couldn't stop shaking with fear and anger. Edeltraut put her arms around me and held me close. "Oh, Irma, Irma," she whispered. I broke down and cried in her arms.

When the sun rose the next morning, I struggled out of the blanket. Ordinarily bright sunlight would have cheered me, but not this morning. I felt as if I had been hit over the head. I was in shock, unable to move, and sick emotionally. All I could do was weep. I wanted to climb into a tub of hot soapy water, but the electricity was out and the pump was frozen.

Edeltraut prepared breakfast and fed the children. I gagged at the thought of food. I just sat in the kitchen crying. The soldiers tramped back inside and roamed around the house. One walked over to me and asked in Russian, "Why are you crying?" I looked at him and thought, *What a question.* He was one of the soldiers who had raped me. *You have to ask that?* I thought without answering. *You have to ask why I am crying?* I choked and wept uncontrollably.

The Russian soldier kept talking softly to me. "You are pretty, Frau," he said. "Come to Russia with me, and I'll be good to you. I'll take care of you. I love you." Everything in me revolted at such a proposal. He was more gentle than the others, and in his way, I suppose, felt sorry for me. But it was like an insult. To go off with a Russian soldier to Russia was the last thing I would do—or so I thought. After a while he left and so did the others.

Fortunately I didn't know what the coming days would bring or I might have been even more agitated. I don't know how I lived through that day and night, but somehow I did. We were left alone that little while, and we began to think we might safely stay in the house. We had swept up the broken dishes and had piled the ruined articles in a corner. All the while near the surface of my thoughts lay the unthinkable. Now I would have a baby, a Mongolian baby, and the trauma was almost more than I could bear.

Our sense of security was short-lived. The next day the soldiers arrived in groups. Whenever we heard horses and a commotion outside, we began to tremble. That day soldiers tried to rape Edeltraut. The children howled and cried when the men tried to take her. With my hands I pointed to Edeltraut and begged them to have mercy. I signed to them that she was pregnant, that she had three small children, and I asked them to please let her go. I pointed to myself. If they had to take somebody, they should take me. I had already been raped so many times. My sign language worked, for they soon left Edeltraut alone. This time Ingrid did not escape.

For once I thanked God Grandma was so confused mentally she didn't understand what was going on. Nor did I. I kept crying in my heart to God and asking, "Why?"

As soon as the soldiers left, my sister said, "It's impossible for us to stay here. We have to get out as fast as we can." While I dressed the children and tried to hurry their grandmother, Edeltraut hitched up the horses. We flung blankets, cooking utensils, and supplies into the wagon. Edeltraut rummaged in the kitchen for matches and candles. By now the wagon was not so heavily loaded. Each time we had stopped, we had discarded some articles or they had been taken from us. As soon as we reached the road, my sister drove the horses at a good clip, while Ingrid and I stumbled along after the wagon.

"Let's go to Tante Hedwig's," Edeltraut said. "It will be a good place to hide. It's off the road and on the edge of the woods." When we reached the house, we found it more wrecked than Edeltraut's house.

"They would find us here, too," Edeltraut said. I could tell she was frantic with worry, not knowing where to go and with the responsibility of all of us on her shoulders. "Wait a minute," she said. "I know another place. Tante Hedwig's neighbor. It's farther in the woods and can't be seen from the road." We started out along a narrow, rutted road that led into the woods. Soon we saw a very small house which looked like a good place to stay.

Vandals had been there, too. Still, we walked inside, cleaned a place to spread our blankets, prepared a little supper, and settled down for the night.

Even now I can't understand why the Russian soldiers had to destroy everything. It was as if madmen had been turned loose in the house, smashing everything in sight. It was like a tornado whipping through the house, leaving walls and roof standing, but smashing and hurling objects with terrific force.

When I thought about how hard our German people had worked for their possessions, about how they had cherished them, I couldn't understand such destruction.

For one night we had peace and quiet. We thought the place was an answer to prayer. In the morning we searched the house for warm clothing and shoes that would fit us. By now Ingrid's and my shoes were ruined from our sloshing along the wet roads. I found a pretty, hand-knit red sweater and put it on. It felt warm and comforting, reminding me of the sweaters my mother had knit for me in the past. I said a quick thank-you to God for the sweater and prayed for my parents, my sister Ruth and brother Kurt, and Helmut, who had been taken from us as a prisoner of war. *Will we ever be together again as a family?* I wondered.

But there was no time to waste on daydreams. The children needed care. Before loneliness and fear could take over, we worked to clean up the kitchen as best we could.

Around noon we sat down for dinner. I had just pulled a meat dish from the wood-burning stove, and Edeltraut was serving the children and their grandmother. Edeltraut stopped, spoon in mid-air.

"Listen!" she said, shushing the children. We all looked at each other as we heard the familiar commotion of soldiers and horses coming up the path. My heart pounded. They had found us after all.

I peeked out the window. "There's a civilian with the soldiers," I said.

"What does that mean?" my sister whispered, looking out the window.

Ingrid's mother said, "He looks like a Russian prisoner now turned traitor. I think he worked at the farm next to ours."

Then the door burst open, and the men tramped into the kitchen. They were better dressed (and their uniforms were cleaner) than most of the Russian soldiers I had seen.

But the commotion made the children cry and clutch their mother. To quiet my own fears I picked up the baby and began feeding him. But a soldier reached over, took the baby from my lap, and handed it to Grandma.

"Put on your coat," he said with a grim-faced look, "and come with us."

I was hungry, but I knew better than to argue with a soldier who had a gun on his shoulder. Over and over I thought, *Where will they take me?*

FIVE
Captured

Before long we learned the civilian's purpose. He spoke German and acted as an interpreter for the Russians, this time for a commission of officers.

"Put on your coat and come with us," the interpreter said to me. And to Ingrid, "Put on your coat."

Thinking of Edeltraut and the children, I took courage and asked, "When will we be back?"

The interpreter turned his head but wouldn't look at me. "Oh! Pretty soon," he said. "In about half an hour or so."

I didn't really trust his words, but I knew better than to refuse to go. Edeltraut would now be left alone with three children, her mother-in-law, and Ingrid's mother, who would help my sister when the new baby's birth was at hand.

"Be good," I told the children. I reached for my coat, pulled on a cap, and made sure I had mittens. With a heavy heart and a backward glance toward Edeltraut, I followed the man out the door. Ingrid walked close behind me.

Outside, a cold March wind whipped across the road. Some of the soldiers tramped before us, others behind us, so we almost ran to keep up. We didn't know what they would do with us or where we were going. If we dared to say a few words to each other, a soldier would thrust a gun in our faces.

Soon we stopped at another house. The interpreter and three officers stalked inside, leaving the others to guard us as we shivered in the cold. In a short while the soldiers and the man hurried out the door with a girl about my age and two boys of eight or nine. Then we marched on, stopping at every house, each time adding more people of all ages.

After several stops I knew I would not be going back to Edeltraut and the children. The truth hit me. *We are prisoners of war.* Fear stalked us every step of the way. *What will they do to us? Kill us?* At fifteen my life lay ahead, and naturally I didn't want to die.

I remembered a Bible verse my parents had taught me: "I can do all things through Christ which strengtheneth me" (Philippians 4:13, KJV). But I didn't feel very strong, nor could I understand why God was letting all this happen to me. Loneliness and hopelessness pressed in on me. I longed to talk to my father and feel my mother's arms around me. *Would I ever see them again?* I prayed my mother wouldn't have to march in the cold. She would never be able to do it.

The sun began to set, and by the time we reached town it was dusk. The soldiers had gathered almost one hundred of us. My feet were soggy wet and aching with cold. I felt stiff and weak since I hadn't eaten for some time.

The officers took us to a house which they used as headquarters. There they registered us by name and questioned us one by one about our families, about whether our fathers and brothers were members of Hitler's *Partei*. At home my parents had taught me strict honesty, so I answered truthfully. But I stressed that my father and brothers had been forced to join the army against their will.

After questioning, they shoved us into a crowded upstairs room. Because it was dark, I had no idea how large the room was. No one could sit down. We stood pressed tight against other people, like on a crowded bus, with no room for our feet to move. The room grew hot and stuffy.

I thought I would suffocate, but I didn't dare take off my coat for fear of losing it in the crowd. It was a wonder someone didn't faint. With the armed guard at the door no one dared to talk.

I didn't know people could treat other

people as we were being treated. The guards yelled at us, pushed us, refused us food and water. I couldn't think of eating, but I was thirsty. When anyone begged for a drink, the guard would say, "Tomorrow." Exhausted from walking and without food, I dozed a little, standing on my feet, wedged in by hot smelly bodies.

In the blackness of the night I heard the guard call my name. "Irma Dreipelcher!" I struggled to the door while he called other names, sixteen in all. Downstairs they took us outside. A glimmer of hope ran through me. *Will we be allowed to go home?* It was dark, and the surroundings were unfamiliar to me. *How will I find my home? Which way will I go?*

Before I could dream anymore, my thoughts were shattered by a shouting guard who lined us up in front of a firing squad. Behind us was an open ditch. *Well, this is it,* I thought. Like a movie put into fast speed, my whole life flashed by—good thoughts of home and family, but also guilt. Why hadn't I listened to my parents and Deacon Kuhn when he had asked me to make a commitment to the Lord? I prayed, *Lord, is it too late for me to be saved?* If I was going to die, I wanted to be ready.

Then several officers from the house walked over to the firing squad. They flashed their lights into our faces and up and down the ditch behind us. They held a discussion with the firing squad. I wondered why we sixteen had been chosen out of all the others. Had it been our answers to the officers' questions? Had I said something wrong or revealed something that angered them? I tried to think back over my answers.

One of the officers who spoke perfect German walked over to us and said, "If you don't tell the truth, you will be shot." I was to learn time after time that when the Russians questioned us, they always did so at night when we were tired and hungry and had been sleeping. I guess they thought they could trick us into telling the truth if we had lied previously.

Now facing death by the firing squad, I thought of how Edeltraut had packed clothes and food and belongings into the wagon when we had tried to escape the Russian army. How important those things had seemed for survival. But when everything is taken and only life is left, then life is the most important. I didn't want to die.

Probably everyone in the group facing the firing squad prayed, but because my parents had taught me to trust God, I felt I had a private line to him. *God, if it is your will that I be shot, I am prepared to die. But if it is not your will, please keep me safe. Thank you, Lord.*

I wondered whether God was punishing me for not having made a decision back there in our kitchen at home. When I had told Deacon Kuhn I wanted to wait, I had thought I had time. I thought I needed an experience to talk about before I could commit my life to Jesus. Now I understood my parents' urgent desire for me to take a stand for the Lord.

As I prayed, I kept thinking, *Lord, I didn't intend such a horrible experience as this.* Gradually God helped me overcome my fears, and peace enfolded me.

After a while the officers began questioning us about our families. Most of the questions were the same as before: What political party had our fathers joined? Had our brothers belonged to Hitler's *Partei?*

I told the truth. "No, they did not belong to Hitler's *Partei,*" I said, stressing again that they had been required to join the army. It was hard for the Russians to believe me because most Germans had joined the Nazi Party.

Suddenly the firing squad put down their guns, and the officers told us to go back to the house, all sixteen of us. We never learned what caused the Russians to change their minds and release us. I only know that God had protected us when we were moments away from death. I was thankful to be alive, and now I was ready for his will in my life.

Inside the house we climbed the stairs to the crowded room. My legs felt rubbery. It was all I could do to reach the top. The guard shouted for those within to make room for us. We pushed in, and the door banged shut behind us.

When daylight came, we saw how small the room was. We also saw that people were jammed into all the rooms upstairs and down. By then we were very thirsty and begged for water, but the guard kept repeating, "Tomorrow." When we were allowed to go outside for toilet purposes, we scooped up snow with our hands and ate it. As soon as the guards caught us, they put a stop to that.

Once while going downstairs, I glanced in a room and saw it was filled with German men, not young people. Wondering whether Helmut was in that room, I lingered and peeked in carefully. I didn't see my brother, but on one side I saw the pastor of Edeltraut's church, lying on the floor.

"Oh, Irma!" he said softly. I nodded and smiled, afraid of being caught. "Yes, yes! Here we are now, Irma," the pastor whispered. "The Lord will be good to us." He quoted a familiar Bible verse that I have forgotten. "God will take care of us." And that was the last I saw of him.

It was God's way, I think, of encouraging me when I was plunged in deep despair, giving me a glimpse of someone I knew. But churning around in my mind was the fear of what was next. They couldn't keep us cooped up in that house for very long. All of us, I think, were expecting something to happen.

SIX
The March to Poland

Early that morning the Russian soldiers herded us outdoors, lined us up in rows six abreast, and commanded us to start marching down the road. We numbered one hundred or more.

Ingrid and I tried to stay together, but not too obviously, or else the soldiers would separate us. They had forbidden all communication between us, but once in a while we managed to whisper a few words.

As soon as the guards moved along the lines out of hearing, an undercurrent of questions surfaced: Where are we going? When will we eat or drink? When will we be warm again? We didn't know the answers, and we didn't dare ask. We knew we were hungry and thirsty, exhausted and cold, and we feared the unknown. If they were going to kill us anyway, why were they waiting?

The spring thaw sent streams of melting

snow down the hills and into the street. Our stockings were wet; our shoe leather was stiff from the moisture. I thought of past days at home after school when I would run from the outside cold into our warm kitchen. If my shoes and stockings had been even damp, I would change into dry ones. I pictured myself cutting a thick slice of homemade bread, pouring a glass of milk, sitting at the kitchen table with my mother, and talking about my school day.

All that seemed so long ago. I wondered whether the tulips had poked their green shoots up through the black soil and snow. I couldn't hold back tears that streamed down my face. Quickly I wiped them away, for I didn't want to stumble in the muddy, slushy road and be stuck with a bayonet or be trampled by other marchers.

At each town soldiers added another fifty or so to the lines—young people, older men, and even children. The towns were bombed beyond recognition. Here and there stood the shells of buildings—some still smoldering—a church perhaps, a house, or a school, now a mass of rubble. I don't know where the people came from, but at each destroyed town a group of prisoners stood waiting.

When it grew too dark to march, the soldiers drove us into a large, cold and drafty building without windows or roof. Of course we had no blankets. Tired as we were, most of us slept only a little that night, huddling together to keep warm.

The next day at the first sign of light, the guards counted us and hustled us into marching formation. We moved at the soldiers' commands like animals driven to market with no will of our own, not knowing our destination. Doubtless, some of the marchers thought of escaping, but where would they go? A run for freedom would mean instant death from a bullet. All we could do was plod along.

A woman behind us said in a low voice, "They added a new marcher to the end of the line. A cow."

"Yes?" someone asked. "How do you know?"

"Word passed along the lines."

"At last we'll get something to eat," a woman said softly. "They'll butcher the cow."

A guard strode toward us, and quickly everyone was silent. I recalled the aroma of beef stew in our kitchen at home. How good that would have tasted now.

But our hopes were crushed. We marched all that second day without food or water. Whenever the soldiers looked the other way or walked down the lines away from us, we resorted to scooping up the dirty snow along the road and eating it. Even though I was without food, the gnawing hunger I first felt gradually left me, but my thirst increased. My mouth felt dry and parched; my lips were cracked and bleeding. I would have traded anything I wore for water.

That night we again slept in a drafty

bombed-out building. Early the next morning while it was still dark, the soldiers roused us. We saw them cooking chunks of the butchered cow in a huge iron kettle. They tossed pieces of the barely warm meat at us, as though we were dogs. Some gnawed at theirs savagely, but I couldn't imagine eating such uncooked, filthy meat, so I refused it. I preferred to go hungry.

Before it was fully light, the guards ordered us into the marching lines. Each time we stopped at a town, the lines grew longer. From time to time new groups of guards replaced the ones we had, so they were rested and fed. On the third day I learned that the best place to march was as close to the head of the lines as possible. People with physical handicaps and those too tired to keep up the pace fell back to the end of the lines. I cringed whenever I heard their cries of pain as the guards beat them and yelled for them to keep up.

Nearly every night the soldiers manhandled some of us girls outside of the building and raped us again and again, leaving us trembling with disgust and with the horrible fear of pregnancy.

On the fourth day rumors filtered along the lines that we were marching to Warsaw, Poland, that our destination was Russia and its slave labor camps.

That day my spirits sank to a new low. *Well, this is the end of Irma,* I thought. Up to then I had had hopes of remaining in Germany and of eventually being reunited with my family. Although I felt depressed, in the back of my mind I felt assured that God would not forsake me. I tried to hold on to that thought.

Ingrid, walking near me, asked, "Why didn't they put us on trains instead of making us walk so far?"

"Not so loud," the woman next to her whispered. "Can't you see the trains and tracks are all bombed out? When we get to Warsaw maybe we'll ride a train." That we did, but what a ride!

My prayers were short those days. Trying to keep up the marching pace took all my energy. But I was sure my parents, wherever they were, would be praying for me. I could just feel their support.

As we plodded along, I comforted myself with the thought that all of us in the lines spoke the same language. Most of the time I was too exhausted to talk or even to think. But at brief moments when we were not under the tightest surveillance I could whisper to a fellow German. As we shivered, hungry and thirsty in the cold, we knew we were suffering together.

I didn't think much about it at the time, but later I realized how good God had been to protect me through those cold and weary days. I didn't catch pneumonia or even a serious cold.

On the fifth day the soldiers boiled a huge kettle of potatoes, skins on. As they roused us to start marching, they yelled, tossed a potato at us, and expected us to catch it. At home I wouldn't have considered a potato with skins on much of a meal. But as my first food in five days it tasted good, and I thanked God for it.

That day we marched through a small town I recognized as Hohenstein-Tannenberg. The town had suffered almost total destruction, but several mausoleums still stood, as did the famous Denkmal, which celebrated Germany's victory in 1914 over Russia. Mausoleums of Kaiser Wilhelm and von Hindenburg were there.

In better days we used to visit my aunts, an uncle, and cousins who lived in the town. *Where are they now?* I wondered. Eagerly I searched the faces of the people added to our marching lines, but recognized no one.

When we reached the border of Poland and looked back at the lines stretching behind us, we couldn't see the end of the marchers. Six abreast, they stretched back too far for us at the head of the lines to be able to see them. Those of us who had marched from the beginning had covered about one hundred miles.

In Poland we were the enemy. Germany had previously captured Poland, and the young generation of Poles hated us. To prevent trouble, security along the lines was tightened.

"Nazis!" they screamed at us. They threw sticks and stones and tried to pull us from the lines to beat us. It was like a riot.

As we trudged along, dragging one foot after the other, I tried to think what my parents would say to me if they were walking beside me. I could see my father at prayer and almost hear him say, "God has not granted us complete knowledge of the future, but he has granted us faith in his grace for each day." I hoped I would live up to my parents' example and teaching. I was fast learning to live one day at a time, trusting God for the future.

I'm not sure how many days altogether we marched. It grew colder the farther north we plodded. When we at last reached Warsaw, guards crowded us into a large building in fairly good condition. With windows and doors intact the building was not as drafty as the other bombed-out places where we had slept—that was something for which to thank God. The officers checked our registrations and searched us. We had to give up everything except the clothes we wore. If any of us had a piece of paper, pencil or pen, scissors, needle, or comb, we had to leave it there.

Day by day I was learning what it meant to be a Russian prisoner of war. Not knowing where we were going or what was ahead kept us in constant despair. Were we really going to the slave labor camps in Siberia?

SEVEN
Starving in a Cattle Car

What happened next turned out worse than anything I had ever dreamed. More than once I looked back on the long march to Warsaw as something better.

The guards hustled us alongside a freight train with many boxcars, which were really cattle cars. They slid open a side door and pushed or dragged about one hundred women and girls into the car. We soon learned to jump when the guards yelled, "Go." The girls who screamed and fought against going into the cattle car paid dearly when the guards struck and kicked them. As soon as one dark, smelly boxcar was filled, the guards would slam the door, lock it, and begin filling another.

As soon as the guards left our car, the girls and women in ours began berating the Russians.

"They ought to be hanged," said one woman, sounding as though she would like to do the job.

"I hope they all starve to death," said another.

"If I had a gun, I'd finish them off—one, two, three," said another girl. "See if I wouldn't."

"Well, you don't have a gun, so quit bragging," Ingrid told her. For a moment I thought the girl would hit Ingrid.

"Keep still," an older woman said. "At least keep still until we start moving and the guards can't hear us. They'd kill us all if they knew what you said."

"I heard Russians don't kill you outright," a little thin girl about my age said. "They just cut off your ears or gouge out your eyes or break your fingers one by one."

Several of the very young girls began to cry. I tried to stop my ears from hearing the horror stories that some people liked to tell. Since I didn't want to be in the midst of all the vicious talk and rumors, I settled into a corner against a side wall.

After what seemed hours, we heard the noise of the locomotive up front. Bumping and jerking cars, the train started off. Soon the inside of the cattle car frosted over with condensation. I began scraping the frost with my fingernails to moisten my lips.

There were too many of us to stretch out to sleep, and with no heat, blankets, or straw on the floor, we bunched together to keep warm.

Privacy was out of the question. A hole cut in the floor of the car with a board to cover it served as a toilet. No one wanted to sleep close to the hole. Those who did suffered greatly from the cold, and doctors later amputated their frostbitten arms and legs.

One morning when I wakened, my braids had frozen tight to the wall. I cried out for help, and two girls came to my rescue. The brittle icy hair broke off easily and I was free. I stared at my long braids frozen against the side of the cattle car, then decided that without a comb it was just as well for me to have short hair.

This trip was the longest of my life. The suspense of not knowing where we were going was part of it. Again and again the train stopped for hours at a time, even a day or two. All this time we had nothing to eat or drink. Our thirst was almost unbearable, and we pounded on the sliding door begging for water.

On the second or third day after we'd begged for the guards to open the door, they finally tossed us a sack of dry bread, two cans of corned beef, and a bag of sugar lumps.

The guards appointed several women as monitors to divide the rations; otherwise there would have been a riot. While the train was stopped with the door open, we looked out across vast stretches of snow. Icy arrows of wind struck us, making us glad when the guards finally slammed the door shut and locked it. Because the smell of the canned meat upset my stomach and my mouth was too dry to eat the bread, I exchanged my portions for extra sugar lumps.

Locked up inside the dark car, without watches or matches, we had no way of knowing where we were or what time it was. On bright days we could see a little light through the chinks. But to sit in the car with nothing to do was physical agony. Rumors flew back and forth, discouraging us. When the train stood still, it was easy for those inside to quarrel and criticize each other.

One woman said, "We're off on a siding. They're going to leave us in this cattle car to die."

"They're shipping us to Siberia," said another, "and will toss us out in the snow to the wolves."

Many thought our plight hopeless and gave up. I might have myself if I hadn't been taught to trust God in all circumstances. Some of us encouraged the others to settle down. We sang old familiar songs and hymns or told stories about our families.

One day a woman named Gertrud said to me, "Irma, I know you."

"How can you?" I asked. "I don't know you."

"You were too little. Do you remember when your parents ran a bakery? I often bought rolls and bread from your mom. You were just a little tyke, but I remember that name—Dreipelcher."

I had thought I was alone among strangers, but God brought my name to Gertrud's mind, and we became friends during the long ride.

Some of us shared recipes with each other and talked about the good meals we used to eat.

"Even the worst meal I had," one girl said, "I'd be satisfied with now."

"When I get home, I'll never complain again about food I don't like," promised another girl.

Whenever the train started, we sighed with relief, though it moved slowly because of the many cars and heavy load of people. But there was something about the rhythm of the train—like a cradle rocking a baby—that made us calm down. Anything was better than sitting still on a siding.

Again I thought back to the time in our kitchen at home when Deacon Kuhn had asked if I was ready to commit my life to Jesus Christ and be baptized, and I had said I wanted to wait. *Wait for a spiritual experience of my own,* I had told myself. Now I was glad my parents didn't know what sort of experience I was having.

I began to feel guilty that I had not committed my life to God at that time. I wondered whether I was paying for not having listened to my parents and Deacon Kuhn. They had known how serious

Germany's plight was and had wanted me to get right with God. But I had only recently told God that I wanted to serve him the best I could. I knew deep down that God loved me, that he was not punishing me, that somehow my experiences would teach me faith and help me grow in my Christian life.

Another problem that plagued me on the long ride was the fear of pregnancy. I kept seeing the Mongolian soldiers who had raped me, and I thought how horrible it would be to have a baby that looked like one of them.

My shyness kept me from talking about my fears to the others. But I prayed day and night and tried to recall Bible verses I had learned in Sunday school. Proverbs 3:5, 6 gave assurance that if I trusted in the Lord, he would direct my paths.

For many in the cattle car the situation appeared hopeless. Still I was silent about my faith in God. In Germany at that time nearly forty years ago, very few were outright Christians, and their faith was private rather than something they talked about to strangers.

Except for Ingrid and Gertrud, I was among strangers. I was a naturally shy girl, and it never occurred to me to speak to strangers or older people about my faith.

In the cattle car the girls and women with no trust in God and with nothing to do thought up evil things to talk about. All of us were depressed, but I, unlike the others, had the Lord to cling to, and he gave me strength day by day. It was never my nature to be depressed for long, and I soon found something to giggle about.

"Look," I told Ingrid, "my stockings are the latest style." What was left of them was full of runs.

We still had nothing to drink, so we begged for water. Finally the guards drew water from the steam locomotive and brought us a pail and a ladle. Greedy ones fought to get near the pail and almost upset it.

"One ladle each," the monitor told us, "or there won't be enough to go around." The few sips we managed to get did little to quench our thirst. Still we were thankful for them.

Our next misery awakened us to action. "Her skin is crawling!" someone screamed, pointing to a young girl. "Look at her head."

"Head lice," said a woman nearby. Others yelled and pulled away from the girl.

"No use," said the woman. "We'll all get them." And we did. Now we had something to occupy us, trying to kill the lice on our heads and bodies as fast as they appeared. Those who were careless suffered great damage to head and body. I remember one girl with patches of her scalp eaten away by the lice.

From time to time someone died. In the morning the guards opened the door and called roll. If anyone failed to respond, a guard picked up the dead body, tossed it out into the snowdrifts, slammed the door, and locked it, leaving the rest of us to wonder who would be next.

Some even wished to die. But life was dear to me at fifteen. With all my heart I wanted to live and see my family again. Somehow I knew they prayed for me every day, and this knowledge gave me the courage to hang on.

EIGHT
Arriving in Siberia

Day after day, week after week, we crowded together in the cattle car, listening to the clackety-clack of the wheels bumping along and the howling of the blizzard outside. At first I didn't know the other women and girls. Gradually I overcame my shyness and made friends with Grete, a girl my age who cried almost every night, and Anna, an older woman who reminded me of a neighbor at home.

I don't know exactly how long we were locked in the cars, but it seemed like a month or more. Then one day the train jolted to a slow stop. We heard voices outside as guards unlocked the doors one by one. We had arrived in Russia. The first stop was Stalinagorsk, a headquarters and prison camp. There we were sorted out and sent to various work camps.

New hope surged within us. "Now they will surely feed us," several women said. "We'll have a chance to stretch our legs and walk," cried one girl. I thought how good it would be to walk in bright daylight again. But our rejoicing soon ended.

The sun shining on the deep snow blinded us so that we couldn't see. As guards shoved us off the cars, we stumbled and fell in the deep snow. I could scarcely stand, let alone walk. Shooting pains and numbness in my legs made me stop to catch my breath. My legs felt paralyzed. For one awful moment I wondered if they were frozen.

The guard yelled at us and prodded us to go on to the headquarters building. So, holding on to each other, staggering and sprawling in the snow, we started out like little children learning to walk. It was a terrifying experience. Those with frozen arms and legs were quickly sent to the hospital for amputations. I almost sang out for joy as soon as I could take a few steps. Again I thanked God for being so good to me. He had spared me from losing legs or arms.

In the camp we hoped to at least have blankets to cover us at night. But there were none, nor mats on the bare bunk boards. *Well,* I thought, *what's new?* I had been sleeping on boards for nearly two months.

In the middle of the night soldiers wakened us, hauled us off to an officer who checked our registrations and questioned us at length. Then doctors examined us. Next women guards deloused our clothes, or so they said. They took us into a room, then told us to strip and hand over our clothes. They hung and jammed the clothing into a big oven so tightly that we found more lice after the delousing than before. Probably the heat of the oven hatched the lice eggs. The women guards kept our bras and girdles, so we had nothing with which to hold up our stockings, not even rubber bands or string.

The shower room was a farce. "Go take a shower," a guard yelled. All I could see was a bowl of water and a small bar of soap. They had to show us what to do. "Soap yourself," said the woman in charge. "Then pour the bowl of water over your head and let it trickle down." A Russian shower! Some of us laughed until we caught the guards eyeing us with malice.

All of us had lost a lot of weight from the march and the poor rations. I had lost my natural plumpness from not eating. Most of us had developed diarrhea and bladder infections, and many could not make it to the outdoor toilets. This enraged the Russians, who cursed us and kicked us around—as though we could help ourselves.

From the time we reached Stalinagorsk, none of us girls menstruated. At first we faced the horror that we were pregnant from the many rapes. But as we talked to the girls who had not been raped (perhaps less than a dozen), they told us they too had stopped getting their period; so we concluded the

Russians had put something in our food.

Some of the girls were already pregnant, and later gave birth to stillborn infants or to babies that lived only a few days. I thanked God that I had been spared such an ordeal.

In the prison camp at Stalinagorsk we did receive food, consisting of two rations a day. In the morning we had a small bowl of souplike hot cereal, and in the evening a bowl of sauerkraut soup. Sometimes if we were fortunate, we would find some fish bones in the soup. Whenever the officers enjoyed fillets from large fish, the bones were added to our soup. Besides the soup or hot cereal we had a chunk of heavy potato bread like none I had ever tasted. I simply could not eat it and would pass it on to someone else. If anyone hoarded a piece for the next day, it would be too moldy to eat. How I longed for the good bread we used to bake at home.

Of course, we whispered among ourselves about the poor rations. One woman said, "Our farmers gave their pigs better food." Bitter hatred against our captors kept some of the women in a bad mood. I lived in a daze from the lack of nourishing food and the shock of seeing others die along the way. Often I felt too exhausted to pray. But I certainly didn't have strength to waste on hating anybody.

After a few weeks the Russians sorted us out for different camps. I don't know how they made the choice. Perhaps they chose young, strong-looking girls and women or those who were not troublemakers. I was young and strong-looking and more mature than some of the other girls.

They packed about three hundred of us into several boxcars. At once rumors flew. "Now we're going back to Germany," one girl said. "Or back to Poland," declared another.

This time we had room to stretch our legs in the dark car. Our hopes rose again, but not for long. When the train stopped, guards hustled us off. We were not in Poland or Germany, but at a place named Schatura, with only a few houses in the middle of the woods, too small to be on a map. I thought we had come to the end of the earth, and so it seemed to be. There was no place to go. Ahead of us lay heavy snow and dense forest. We stumbled in the drifts, and icy whips of wind stung us. Our feet and legs suffered most. We still wore the same clothes we had started out with a few months before.

Guards ordered us to start marching ahead. Soon in a clearing we saw new barracks surrounded by a high fence and a locked gate. At each corner of the fence a shedlike tower housed an armed guard with a powerful searchlight, making escape impossible, if one were foolish enough to try it. Men and boys were housed in one barracks; women and girls in another.

Inside the women's barracks, which had upper and lower bunks, a small heater stood in one corner, not nearly sufficient to warm the big barnlike structure.

"Look," my friend Anna said, "you can see right through the cracks in the boards." Sure enough. The barracks must have been put up hastily from new boards that were still wet and frost-covered.

As before, the bunks held no blankets or mats, just icy bare boards, though the guards promised us blankets soon. We crowded around the stove for a little warmth until a guard strode in and ordered us to climb into the bunks and sleep. "Tomorrow you go to work," he said.

Some of the girls started squabbling about who would sleep in the top bunks, which would be a little warmer than the lower ones and would give a view of the whole barracks. My months as a Russian prisoner had taught me to look out for myself, so I quickly climbed onto a top bunk.

Before we fell asleep that night, the truth hit us. "This is Siberia," Anna said soberly.

"Yes," another agreed, "a slave labor camp in Siberia."

The chill that ran through me was more penetrating than the cold.

NINE
Slave Labor

The next morning, shivering and stiff from the cold, we crowded near the stove in the corner. Those in the back tried to elbow their way closer to the heat. But the pushing and shoving were only half-hearted because most of us were weak and famished.

I stared at a girl named Frieda. When we had first entered the cattle car, she had been well built like me, but now her clothes were several sizes too large and hung on her. Her round face and pink cheeks had now become gaunt and ashen. Without a mirror I could only guess at my own appearance. I knew I, too, had lost weight because my arms and legs and body were very thin.

"Will they leave us here to freeze to death?" cried Frieda.

"Remember all those trees in the forest?" Ingrid asked. "Plenty of wood to keep us warm."

"Who's going to chop down trees?" jeered Frieda. "Not those lazy guards." And she was right.

"Forty below zero," a girl said.

"How do you know?" asked Ingrid.

"I heard the guards talking."

Outside the wind howled, and icy blasts blew in through the cracks in the wall. German winters never grew that cold. How would we keep warm? We soon found out. Guards tramped into the barracks with piles of used quilted clothing—coats, padded trousers, caps, mittens, quilted boots—and dropped them, along with rubber boots, onto the floor. We grabbed whatever we could reach.

"At last the Russians are showing us a little kindness," I said.

"With these old rags?" asked Anna, holding up a jacket with a long rip in it.

"Look how dirty they are!" cried Frieda.

Tattered, ripped, and filthy, the clothes had evidently been discarded on some garbage heap by the Russians. Yet we were expected to wear these rags. With the soldiers ordering us outside we quickly pulled on the quilted clothing, feeling somewhat warmer, but not for long. The meaning of a slave labor camp in Siberia began to sink into our lives. They separated us into small groups with one guard for each group, marched us to the woods, and showed us hatchets, axes, and saws.

"Chop!" yelled the guard, pointing to the

big trees and dense underbrush. The foreman signed to us to clear away the undergrowth with hatchets so we could get at the tree trunks.

At home I had known what it meant to work hard, but I had never chopped down a tree of any size, let alone a big one. Some of the tree trunks were too large for two of us to circle with our arms. Others were birch trees two feet or so in diameter.

At first we could scarcely lift the heavy axes, but with the guard yelling at us, we quickly learned how to swing one, a girl working on each side of a tree trunk. When a tree was ready to topple, the supervisor gave the signal, and we watched the tree crash to the ground.

Then we trimmed off branches and set them aside in a pile. Next with two working on a crosscut saw, we cut the tree into about five-foot logs. Two girls would hoist a log onto their shoulders and then, staggering under the weight, would carry it out to the clearing.

The foreman assigned a quota to each group of four to six girls. We worked as fast as possible so that we could finish and rest a little. But we learned that the faster we worked, the more the quotas increased day by day.

Whenever a guard turned his back or we carried the logs to the clearing, we whispered.

"A log this size would warm the barracks," I said, trying to balance my end of the heavy log.

"Too green," the girl at the other end whispered. "It wouldn't burn." Then since we needed all our strength to plow through the deep snow, we kept still. Because no beaten path led back to the clearing, we often sank in snow to our waists and had to struggle to get out. We never learned what happened to the big logs we chopped and sawed into lengths.

Clearing the forest consumed all my strength. At night I could barely stumble back to the barracks. Sore muscles and aching back cried out for a hot bath. *Wake up, Irma,* I told myself. *You're not at home in East Prussia. This is Siberia.* I drank the thin soup they gave us and dragged myself onto the top bunk, utterly exhausted.

But one more job awaited us before we could sleep. Sitting cross-legged on our bunks, we deloused ourselves and each other in an effort to keep clean. Once I looked over at Ingrid and laughed. "Just like monkeys in the zoo," I said. But Ingrid didn't think it was funny.

By now we had straw mats covered with thin cloth sacks on our bunks. Out of necessity we ripped away pieces of the sacks to use for undergarments. The Russians wondered why the sacks were becoming shorter and shorter. We slept about fifteen in long bunks, close together to keep warm.

Sometimes a woman would be saying the rosary, and another would start humming a hymn. Soon we would all join in before drifting off to sleep.

One morning Frieda let out a small shriek and jumped out of the bunk. She pointed to the girl next to her and said, "She's dead." When the guard came in, he dragged the body outside and stored it in a shedlike building.

"Typhus," Anna said without emotion, "from bad water." Officers had warned us about typhus symptoms telling us to report at once to headquarters. Still the disease spread, and many girls and women in our camp died during those cold months.

Again I praised God for protecting me against illness, even when the girl next to me died of typhus. He graciously threw a protective shell around me, a sort of emotional numbness, so that I witnessed death and suffering but felt no heart-wrenching scars. Even when we walked over to the shed where they stacked the dead bodies to see if anyone we knew was the latest casualty, I felt no deep sadness. I fought to exist, and my emotions lay dormant.

In the concentration camp, I grew vaguely aware of my fellow slaves. The youngest was a three-year-old girl whose mother bundled her up each day and lugged her along to the forest. The oldest was an eighty-year-old woman, thin and bent. She reminded me of Edeltraut's confused mother-in-law, but this old one was alert and often hummed bits of a hymn in a weak voice. When I was not too tired to listen, the songs comforted me. I took her feeble music to be a sign of hope from God. Surely he would bring me safely out.

Each week we saw new barracks built to accommodate more and more prisoners. As spring came and the snow thawed, guards ordered us to dig drainage canals. Day after day we plodded a little farther into the swampy peat moss the Russians used to generate electricity. The guards threw birch logs here and there across the drainage canals for us to go back and forth.

"I'll fall in," Ingrid wailed, a guard poking her with a gun.

"Run!" he spit out. We had to learn to run fast across the logs for fear of toppling into the deep water. One old woman, afraid of falling, had trouble balancing herself. The guard pushed her, and she fell into the ditch—the last we saw of her.

Our thirst was so great that at times, against strict orders, we would fearfully scoop up a handful of the murky brown canal water and drink it.

We could tell what the day would be like by the guard in charge. Young men worked us hard, and women guards had no mercy. If anyone tried to sit down and rest a few minutes, the guard would pounce on us with a rifle and whack us across our backs. "You have a quota to fill," he'd tell us. But if an older man was in charge, the day might be fairly easy. I remember one older man who encouraged us to sit down for a short while.

"Take it easy," he said. "Tomorrow is another day." Then he shared his lunch with us. He made me think of my father. Such a surge of love and homesickness welled up within me that I prayed briefly that God would somehow pull me out of this mess and unite me with my family again.

The summer months were humid and as hot as the winter months were cold. On days when someone was too sick to go with the others to dig, she remained in the barracks. But that turned out to be almost as bad as the woods or swamps. She had to clean the barracks or sweep the camp. Rest was out of the question.

Occasionally some of us would be picked to work in the kitchen. To see and smell the good food prepared for the soldiers tormented us, starved as we were.

"They wash the dishes and give us the dishwater for soup," Frieda said spitefully. I had to agree that our food was very poor and scant. Often I couldn't tolerate even a spoonful of what the guards brought us to eat, so I'd give my portion to someone who'd eagerly take it.

On the way to the outdoor toilets I passed the dump where the kitchen help threw the dishwater and any garbage left from the officers' tables. One day a sick man lay stretched out on the ground near the dump, groping for discarded potato peels and scraps of food.

"Go back to the barracks," I pleaded with him. "If the guards see you, they'll put you in prison."

He looked at me out of almost sightless eyes. "Prison?" he repeated feebly.

My words did sound silly because we already were in prison, but the guards had a worse punishment and a worse place for those who disobeyed rules. I knew all about that solitary confinement. One time when I was working in the kitchen, I returned to the barracks with a big handful of raw potato peelings. Frieda, Ingrid, and I spread them on top of the stove, trying to cook them. We weren't too successful. The peelings tasted rough and scratchy as we ate them. But that wasn't the worst. A guard appeared, shouted at us, and took us off to prison confinement. While we were there, the guards pulled us into a storeroom and raped us.

Because I thought the man lying beside the dump had suffered enough, I tried to help him back to the men's barracks, but he refused to go. The next time I went outside he was gone.

Day by day I grew thinner and weaker. When I looked at myself, I thought, *Irma, you are skin and bones, a walking skeleton.* Had God brought me through such horrible experiences just to let me die there in Siberia? Somehow I knew he must have a purpose for allowing me to live this long.

TEN
A Glimpse of Russian Life

After our meager evening rations we had nothing to do but crawl into our bunks and fall asleep. One night a minister's wife, also a prisoner, sat on the floor holding a small black book in her hands. She beckoned some of us nearer.

"See!" she said softly. "A New Testament with Psalms."

"Where did you get it?" asked several of us.

"Shh!" she replied, looking over her shoulder at the door where a guard might enter at any time. "Smuggled it."

"How?" I wanted to know. "They made us give up everything but our clothes when we got here."

The woman smiled gently. "God helped hide it for me" was all she would say.

"Read something," pleaded a girl.

Quietly the woman read the twenty-third

Psalm. From memory I repeated the words along with her. Our family had often used that psalm in our devotions.

"May I see it?" asked one of the older women. She held it lovingly, fingering the pages carefully. "What I wouldn't give for a Bible to read these days." After a moment she returned the New Testament to the minister's wife, who took the book, opened it, and reverently ripped out page after page, passing them around to all of us. Some of the women wept with joy. Others looked at their page curiously. Perhaps they had never seen a Bible before.

My page was from the Psalms. The words of one verse jumped out at me: "This poor man cried, and the Lord heard him, and saved him out of all his troubles" (Psalm 34:6, KJV). I took the words as a direct promise that God would help me.

For several days we secretly read our portions of Scripture, but nothing could be kept secret from the guards for very long. Soon a grim-faced soldier grabbed the hidden pages from us and destroyed them.

At night some Catholic women in the barracks prayed aloud with their rosaries and sang "Hail, Mary." We joined them, and even unbelievers were drawn toward thoughts of God and religion.

I have often wished now that I had been bolder those days in my Christian witness. But in Germany Christians had lived for years under Hitler's threat of arrest for attending church. He had wanted people to go Sunday mornings to his *Partei* meetings, instead. I had been conditioned to keep quiet about God, avoiding talk about my religion.

After the guard destroyed our Scripture pages, I tried to recall Bible verses I had learned in Sunday school. No matter what the Russians did to me they could never take away those verses. They were mine.

Because of weakness from lack of food, I was relieved from going out to dig ditches. Instead, my assignment was to clean the officers' barracks outside our camp. For the first time since the Russians captured me I saw beds with mattresses and blankets and sheets. But I also saw the unbelievable filthiness of those Russian soldiers. The floors were covered with spit. The men ate sunflower seeds and spit the shells on the floor. Anything else they didn't want landed there, too.

That first morning I thought the place hadn't been cleaned for months. I couldn't see a pail or mop or scrub brush, so I stood helpless. When an officer walked by, I asked how I was to clean the barracks without a mop and a pail. By now I could understand and speak a number of Russian words. The officer showed me the pump, then cut some birch branches from the nearby woods and tied them together into a makeshift broom. When I returned with a pail of water, I knelt to scrub the floor.

"No! No!" he cried. He swept some of the

debris out the door. Slopping a little water on the floor, he put his foot on the birch broom and scrubbed back and forth with it. Thus I learned how to scrub with my foot.

By the end of the day I had cleaned the officers' barracks. Scarcely able to drag myself back to my own barracks, I took comfort in the thought that tomorrow would be easier. When I returned the next day to clean the officers' quarters, I couldn't believe my eyes. The floor was as filthy as the day before.

The work wasn't a great deal lighter than digging ditches, but it did bring extra benefits. Sometimes an officer gave me a piece of bread, better tasting than the soggy potato bread we received. Once in a while an officer gave me a bar of soap. I hadn't seen a bar of soap in months. How good it felt to wash with soap. I passed it around so the other women in my barracks could use it, too.

A short distance outside the high board walls around our concentration camp stood other barracks, a camp for Russian girls and women. They had been captured by the Germans and had worked on German farms or in industries. Recaptured by the Russians, they had to serve a one-year prison term, working hard as punishment for having worked for the Germans. They made the best of their sentence. Often when I walked back in the evening after a day spent cleaning the officers' quarters, I would hear the Russian girls singing and dancing, their heavy boots clumping on the wooden floors.

For good behavior some of us were assigned to work outside our fenced-in barracks. We walked as close to the Russian girls' building as we dared. The girls, dressed in dull, gray quilted trousers and long jackets, even in warm weather, ran toward us. Some of the German girls had had the time before being captured to put on several layers of clothing. Quite a few still had yellow, blue, or red sweaters and blouses. The Russian girls liked the bright colors and begged for our sweaters, offering bread in exchange. Since our rations were scant and our prison bread so sickening, we gladly exchanged clothing for bread.

Back in our barracks Ingrid said, "I wish I had all the sweaters I left at home to exchange for their bread."

"What will we do when we run out of sweaters?" I asked. "Maybe we can unravel a sleeve and knit a small scarf or mittens and make the yarn last longer."

"Where will we get knitting needles?" Frieda asked.

"Let's look outside for wire," Anna suggested. It was hard to find stiff wire, but we scrounged around, found a few pieces, and sharpened the ends on a stone. The Russian girls were just as pleased with mittens or a scarf as with a whole sweater.

As we walked through the nearby town on our work crews, we passed houses built of logs. The logs were held together by mudlike clay with cotton string rolled up into balls and stuck into the plaster to give it body. Here and there the cotton string stuck out of the mud plaster in tuftlike bunches.

"Look at the white string," Frieda whispered to us. She walked close to a house, reached out, and yanked a tuft of string. It came out easily. Later in the barracks we crowded around Frieda and watched her pull the soft string apart into lengths of three to five feet.

"It would be good for knitting," I said, fingering the string. "We could use it with the colored yarn from our sweaters and make the yarn last longer."

The next time we walked to town several of us grabbed wads of the white string. As long as we passed the log houses on our work assignments, we kept up our supply of white cotton string. I don't know what happened to the log cabins.

With fall approaching, the days grew colder, and we again put on the quilted clothing discarded by the Russians. One day an officer asked for volunteers to help out on the farm.

"Volunteers?" Frieda whispered. "Is it a trap? Will they take us out there and leave us to die?"

"Not me," Anna said. "I know what it's like here. Who knows what we'll have to do on a farm."

"It can't be any worse than what we're doing now," I said. "I'm going to volunteer."

The new work meant we marched a long way to a place where mushrooms and berries and vegetables grew. We learned that Russian farming was different from ours in Germany where each farmer planted and harvested his own crops. In Russia the farms joined together and were tended and harvested as a commune. Workers piled the potatoes, cabbages, and carrots in one place for later distribution.

How long had it been since we had eaten fresh berries and vegetables? Months and months. We wiped the dirt off the carrots and stuffed ourselves greedily as we picked berries, dug potatoes, and pulled carrots. Eating nourishing food those days brought new strength and encouraged us.

We counted ourselves fortunate to have a kind older guard who looked the other way when we ate carrots or berries. We packed carrots into our quilted boots to take to the barracks. On the long walk back we must have waddled like ducks, but we made it and divided the carrots with others in camp.

With the approach of the long winter months, we were again herded to the forest to chop more trees. As we sawed birch logs, we cut off thin slices of the tree, hiding them in our quilted trousers. Back in the barracks we made plaques to hang on the wall and breadboards, though we had no bread to slice. Pencils occasionally turned up in the barracks, perhaps from the Russian girls. One of our girls with artistic ability drew flowers on the birch wood and sometimes added a Bible verse. The Russian girls eagerly exchanged food for the breadboards and plaques and even paid us Russian money. We could use the money to buy things at the bazaar, or farmers' market, outside our camp.

One bitter cold day after a blizzard, the guards assigned us in work crews of six to ten to go to the nearby town and shovel the streets. Because of the cold my face froze, and my hands felt as stiff as ice. Using my frozen face as an excuse to go to the side, I tried to rub some life into my cheeks with a handful of snow.

When a guard turned his back, I left the crew. Fully knowing the risk I took, I dared to escape from the group to warm up. Those days I lived for the present, not thinking much about the past or too much about the future. I was freezing with cold and I wanted to get warm. Within arm's length I saw the door of a house, opened it, and quickly slipped inside. Several chickens and goats greeted me with an uproar. *Oh, please be quiet!* I thought. *If the guard hears and investigates, I'll be shot.* Inside the room several children turned to quiet the chickens and goats.

Doubtless, I frightened the children, who recognized me as a German, an enemy, a prisoner. They made a worse uproar than the chickens and goats. They swore at me, shouted Russian words, and pelted me with wooden dishes, shoes, and other objects.

I put up my arms trying to dodge the missiles and looked around. The kitchen held a big oven and fireplace. Above the huge brick oven the Russians made their bed with straw and blankets. *If I could crawl into that warm bed,* I thought, *I would go to sleep and not wake up for a long time.* But such a dream didn't last, for I was literally kicked out of the house. The lovely warmth of the kitchen tempted me not to give up, and I entered the next house.

A woman stood at the table making Russian pies. When she saw me, her mouth opened in surprise. Then she picked up her rolling pin. Before she could clobber me with it, I used a few Russian words to quiet her.

"Don't be afraid," I told her. "I'm cold and all I want is to warm up a little." I did not dare say I was hungry, too, because I had to return to the work crew before they missed me.

Greatly upset, the woman pointed to three pictures on the wall, probably her husband and sons. "Hitler! Hitler!" she repeated over and over, her eyes blazing with hatred. She must have hated me, too, because she knew I was a German, and the Germans had deprived her of her husband and sons.

"War is wrong," I signed to her, showing that I agreed. "Hitler is bad. But I am just a young girl and not to blame for what Hitler did." I pointed to the pictures and told her I was sorry for her loss.

She must have understood a little of what I said, for she calmed down, pointed to the stove, and continued filling her pies with a mixture of sauerkraut and beets. I stood near the stove, letting the heat warm me and thinking that not all Russians were bad. Some didn't like the horrors of war any more than I did. In a moment I thanked her and quickly left.

When I rejoined the street-shoveling crew, the guard had been busy overseeing the other crews and hadn't missed me. Once more God's protective care encouraged me.

As the hot summer months rolled around again, my throat refused to swallow the poor rations we received, and my weight kept going down. At times I couldn't walk by myself or lift my head from the bunk bed. I was of no use to anyone and had no hope of ever getting out of Siberia. As I lay in my bunk, I was sure I had come to the end of my life. I prayed and again told God that I belonged to him and was willing to accept whatever he wanted for me, even if it meant death. All I wanted was his will. Gradually his peace comforted me.

One day when I must have been on the verge of starvation, two girls stood beside my bunk with a tin cup of watery soup.

"Here, Irma, eat this," one said.

"I can't swallow the rotten stuff," I replied.

"Even if it's not good," the girl said, "eat to keep up your strength."

I shook my head.

"Irma," the other girl said, "you want to go home and see your family, don't you? Not just die here?"

A shudder traveled down my spine. With all my being I wanted to be released, but wasn't that hopeless?

"Eat for strength," the girl repeated, holding the tin cup to my lips. With a sigh I reached for the cup and gulped down the watery soup.

It was a turning point. The girl's words "You want to see your family, don't you?" rang in my ears a long time. With much difficulty I managed to eat a little food each day. By degrees I gained some strength, but not any weight that I could tell. It was not my nature to stay depressed, and I tried to make the best of my circumstances.

ELEVEN
The Train on the Other Track

Late in August the women in charge assigned some prisoners extra work duty. For days they swept and scrubbed and cleaned. The barracks buzzed with rumors.

"Who's coming?" we wanted to know.

"A commission of doctors from Moscow," someone replied. We seldom believed the rumors, but this time we could tell something important was going to happen.

"Doctors!" sputtered Frieda. "It's about time. Look how thin we are. We're dying of malnutrition."

"Do you suppose they'll send us to another camp where we won't have to work so hard?" I felt sorry for the woman who had just spoken. She was quite old and shaky. Many times she fell down at work and needed help standing again. A number of the rest of us were too weak to work at all.

"I heard they are going to release us," a

girl said. Her words raised a clamor of voices.

"How do you know?" "When will we go?" "How will we go home?" When we dared to question the guards, they answered with a grin, "Tomorrow." We didn't trust them because they had lied so often, but this time we wondered if it might be true.

The news of release, a straw to clutch at, helped us endure the dreary days of waiting for the commission of doctors from Moscow. The day they arrived we lined up outside the barracks used as the doctors' office. We had to undress outside and file past the doctors, about six or eight of them. I was skin and bones and too exhausted to be embarrassed about nakedness. When it was my turn to be examined, the doctor wrote on the report: *Weight—seventy-five pounds.* That didn't surprise me.

One doctor scowled and said, "They're of no use. Send them home."

Back in the barracks we talked more than we had for a long time. "Is the war over?" we wondered. We had heard no outside news and did not know what was going on in the world. "Are we going home to Germany?" the girls asked. We couldn't believe it after the long months spent in Siberia.

It was close to a year and a half since the Russians had snatched me from my sister's family and had made me a slave in Siberia. Lately in my weak condition I hadn't thought much about my parents or my brothers and sisters. Now homesickness surged through me. I longed to be with them, to feel my mother's arms around me, to hear my father's kind voice. Yet when I thought of how I looked, I wanted to spare them the pain of seeing me. I began to cry—something I hadn't done in a long time.

Before packing us into the train of cattle cars, the guards gave us a warning speech. I knew enough Russian to understand them. "You're going home. This time the doors will remain open, unlocked. Nobody is to leave the train. You'll be shot if you do."

"Going home?" asked Ingrid. "I don't believe it."

"Neither do I," another girl said, shivering with fear. "They're going to put us in another camp for the rest of our lives."

Gradually peace settled over me, as if God had spoken, "Irma, you are going home." Then I knew why I hadn't been able to eat much those long months. If I had stayed well and strong as some of the others, I wouldn't be on the train leaving Siberia. With all my heart I praised God for curbing my appetite while there. My weakness and emaciated appearance made up my passport to freedom.

As the engine picked up speed, the forests and wide open spaces seemed to slide by. When the train finally stopped, we acted like animals locked up too long, jumping down from the cars and running into the fields.

"Look at the cabbages," cried one woman. We grabbed the big heads, tore them apart, and ate the juicy green leaves. As soon as the guards realized we had left the cars, they yelled, waved their guns, and herded us back into the freight train.

"Next time we shoot to kill!" they shouted. "And lock the doors." But Russian rules didn't mean much to us then. We were not thinking ahead. We were starved, and fresh vegetables tasted good.

Into my mind flashed the picture of the starving Russian prisoner outside my mother's hospital room in East Prussia. I recalled how deeply stirred I had been when the prisoner had scooped up some of the chicken scraps. Now I was the hungry one, and I had dared to snatch what was forbidden. Then I remembered my mother's words: "It is not right. God will not leave such acts unpunished."

But in the freight car I couldn't see much sense in wasting time thinking about how God would punish such cruelty. I had more important ideas to consider.

We were going home, but we couldn't be sure where our homes were. I knew bombs had destroyed all of East Prussia where I had once lived. At the time of my capture my family was scattered. Where were they now? Where would I go? Where was home?

Finally we pulled into a large city station, probably Moscow, where our train sat idle for a while. Other trains kept coming and going on both sides of us. All at once an express train drew up next to us, and we could look into the dining car.

"Frieda," I cried, pointing to the windows. "Look at all the scraps of food left on the table, and no people in the dining car."

Frieda looked in the windows, then at me. We had the idea at the same time. While both trains were stationary, we jumped out of our car and ran up the steps to the dining car. Quickly we gathered into napkins all the scraps of bread and meat and potatoes. Frieda kept searching tables a little farther in the dining car.

"Come on," I begged, "before we get caught." I ran off the express train with Frieda following. We knew we were stealing and disobeying rules, but we didn't care. The sight of good food, even scraps, did something to our hunger, and we couldn't resist.

Outside I heard the noise of our train pulling away. "Frieda!" I screamed. "Our train is moving. It's going to leave without us." The train was fifty feet down the track and picking up speed. We ran as fast as we could, still clutching the scraps of food. Little by little we gained on the moving freight cars. I thought my chest would burst open from running so fast.

At last we caught up and flung ourselves into the open door of the moving train. For a few minutes I lay on the floor, oblivious to those around me, my heart thumping in my throat as I tried to catch my breath. At the same time I saw the express train speeding off in the other direction. I pushed the napkin of scraps over to the others, for I had completely lost my appetite. I shuddered with fright for what might have happened, and for some time I lay in a daze. Gradually I realized how daring I had been, heedless of the consequences.

What if we had failed to catch up to our train and it had left without us? Surely they would have shipped us back to Siberia. I felt ashamed for having disobeyed rules and for having taken the leftover food. I prayed for forgiveness and promised God I wouldn't leave the train until we reached our destination. Oh! how I thanked him that we had reached our car in time. From then on I began to think seriously of what it really meant to trust God.

As we rode along, we kept watching for signs of our native land. Because of the bombing and destruction some towns were being totally rebuilt, so we couldn't recognize any familiar landmarks. Once in the early morning hours our train carried us through a city, close to houses. Through the lighted windows we saw families eating breakfast and preparing to go to work. We judged the town to be Berlin.

"Oh! They have lamps," Frieda cried.

"They have tables and dishes," another girl said.

"They have beds with pillows and

blankets," I added. Because we had been deprived of such common necessities for months, we had almost forgotten they were a part of daily life.

After many days, we arrived in Frankfurt (Oder) where we stayed in quarantine for about two weeks. Then they transferred us to Camp Ruedersdorf in East Berlin, an occupation camp. Those in charge explained that we were free to go home as soon as we found relatives to sponsor us. How could we do that? We had no idea where any of our relatives were. We were truly displaced persons.

Sitting in that camp day after day brought me a new sense of defeat and restlessness. Had I been released from Siberia only to be held in an occupation camp in Germany? One by one some of my friends located family members and left Camp Ruedersdorf. But I found no trace of my family. Since I couldn't endure the waiting, I stopped at the office to check in for a job.

"I want to volunteer for work," I said.

The man in charge looked at me and grunted. "What can you do? Only jobs we have are housework. Can you do that?"

"Yes, of course," I said, willing to try.

He handed me an address in Schoeneiche (East Berlin), and I set out on foot. The man of the house owned a grocery store, the wife was in the hospital dying of cancer, and a nineteen-year-old daughter worked as a medical technician.

"You don't look very strong," the man said when he saw me.

"I know how to cook and clean," I said.

"Well, you'll have to take charge of the household. My wife is in the hospital, and I'm busy in the grocery store."

At sixteen I didn't know much about managing a household, but I was eager to learn, and anything was better than sitting in camp waiting for the unknown.

When the man's daughter came home from work that night, she looked at me with shock and pity. Going into her room, she returned with an armful of clean clothes.

"Here," she said. "You can have these if they fit." Thankfully I assured her they would fit. "Come," she said, "I'll show you the bathtub." She filled the tub with hot water and laid out a towel. "Put your old clothes outside the door."

"Thank you," I said, my eyes brimming with tears at her kindness. I never saw my ragged clothes again. The girl probably burned them.

For a long time I soaked in the tub of soothing warm water and fragrant soap, my first real bath in eighteen months. In my new home I had a room of my own, a bed with a feather tick, a brush and a comb, a toothbrush. What luxuries! When I put my head on the down pillow that night, I thanked God for his goodness.

Preparing meals took all my strength. The family kept the potatoes in the cellar. The first time I walked down the steep steps I could scarcely lift the basket upstairs. I climbed one step at a time, lifting the basket and resting on each step. I began to realize how weak I was.

My work took planning, too. We had ration cards for our meat and other groceries. The amount of food we could buy was very meager and had to last the week. Most of our supplies came from the man's grocery store and from his sister who gave us fruit and vegetables from her orchard and garden.

I began to eat and eat. My stomach was without a bottom, I thought, since my hunger was never quite satisfied. As I gained weight, my strength increased, but I also grew puffy. Most of the girls who had been taken to Siberia still had not menstruated. I visited a doctor who gave me injections to start my period, and before long I felt normal again.

How good the Lord was to lead me to this family that trusted me as one of their own, helping me regain strength and confidence. Still deep inside I missed my own family. I felt that some of them must be alive, and I grew restless to find them. Daily I prayed that God would lead me to them, or at least give me news of what had happened to them.

TWELVE
Search for Family

All the while I worked in Schoeneiche the desire to find my own family lay uppermost in my mind. On shopping trips, standing in line for ration cards, or walking along the street for exercise, I talked to others released from prison camps.

"Have you found your family?" I'd ask. Usually the answer was yes. They had found a brother or sister, a parent or child, and would soon leave to join them. I grew impatient. Somehow I knew that working for this good family was only temporary. I had to find my parents, my brothers and sisters, if they still lived. Because I believed that all things were possible with God, I had faith that he would lead me to them.

I became close friends with Gertrud, a girl who worked for a nearby family and bought groceries in my employer's store. She had also been a slave in Siberia, and was trying to find her family. We were about the same size and both had fair skin and blonde hair. People often mistook us for sisters.

One Sunday when we had free time, I said to Gertrud, "Let's take the streetcar to Berlin and go window-shopping."

"Let's!" Gertrud was enthusiastic.

We dressed, brushed our hair, and put on makeup—something we had not done for a long time. We giggled at our pink cheeks and red lips.

Peering into the mirror, Gertrud said, "We look like circus clowns."

I had to agree. "Let's wipe some of it off."

Finally we set out for the streetcar ride to Berlin. Although we had never been there before, our past experiences had given us confidence to make the trip. We didn't think about a special place to go. We only wanted to explore, look in the store windows, and have a good time.

The streetcar bumped along the uneven tracks, stopping to take on more passengers as we neared town. Many people were at work on the brick walls and steps of houses, repairing bombed-out buildings. Others had put up temporary shelters. As the streetcar stopped in a suburb of Berlin to discharge passengers, I had a strong impulse to get off.

"Quick!" I told Gertrud. "Let's get off here." We hopped off. Looking up and down the street, we saw people going into a building. I didn't know what kind of building it was or what we would find. But if so many others were going in, there must be something interesting inside. So we followed the crowd. As we reached the doorway, I saw a small sign that read "Baptist Church."

"Oh!" I stopped short. "A church. Just like home. Let's go in," I told Gertrud. Although I had asked several people about a Baptist church, there wasn't one in the little town where I worked. The family I worked for didn't go to church and had no Bible in their home.

Gertrud and I followed the others, walking through a short archway to a small chapel-like building with benches. We never would have found it on our own. We slipped into the back bench, listened to the hymns, Scripture, and sermon. The minister, gray-haired with a deeply lined face, reminded me of my father. I hoped we could talk to him because I thought he would be kind and understanding.

As I sat with other believers who were warm and friendly and heard the Word of God, my emotions were touched. I thought of the church at home where I had gone as a child, and I began to weep. I was starved for Christian fellowship and the Bible.

Through the whole service I cried out of gratitude that God had found this church for me. He had directed me to take the streetcar ride. He had impelled me to get off at a certain street and follow the crowd into the church.

After the service the pastor spoke to us. "Have you girls been here long?" he asked. "What are your names?"

"I'm Irma Dreipelcher," I said, then introduced Gertrud.

"Dreipelcher," the pastor repeated. "That sounds familiar. Do you have a relative named Karl Dreipelcher?"

"Oh, yes," I replied. "He's my uncle. He had a big farm in East Prussia."

"Well, well," the pastor said. "All through the war my children spent summer vacations on your uncle's farm. His farm fed many children of ministers."

I couldn't believe that the first person I met in the city knew some of my family. The pastor, laughing and joking, put his arm around my shoulders and led us to his study. He talked about my family, about where we had been and what we needed. I said I had nothing but what the family I worked for had given me. But most of all I longed to find my own family.

"Well, girl," he said, "with a large family like yours we will surely find some of them." He reached for two big books on his desk. "See," he said. "The Baptist church put together these directories for missing persons. People come in and look over the lists to find their families. Anyone can come and look up relatives, and many have found their loved ones." He handed me one directory and Gertrud another. My fingers trembled so that I could scarcely open the directory.

With rising excitement I ran my fingers down the pages. Were my parents still alive? Would I find their names listed?

All at once I stopped. "There," I whispered. "Marie Dreipelcher. My mother's name." Overcome with tears of joy I could scarcely speak.

"Here," said the minister, handing me pencil and paper.

My hands shook so that I had difficulty copying the address. As I kept searching the directory, I found the names of my brother-in-law and a cousin, but not my father's. I wanted to take the next streetcar back so I could write to my mother.

"Wait," the pastor said, pulling a carton from under the table. "Every so often people in America send us a box of used clothes and shoes to distribute to needy persons. I can't think of anyone more needy than you two girls. Take the carton with you."

The box held dresses and underclothing, shoes and stockings, sweaters and purses. Gertrud and I divided the clothing and thanked the minister for his kindness.

"Who are these good people?" I asked. "I'd like to write and thank them."

The minister shook his head. "We don't know. They never send their names."

Back at the home where I worked I told of my visit to the church and showed them the box of clothes from America. They could hardly believe such generosity. I explained about finding my mother's name in the directory and wanting to write to her as soon as possible.

My employer's daughter put her arm around me. "Irma, I'm happy you found your mother. But I know what that means. You'll soon leave us. We're sorry and we'll miss you very much." I told her I, too, would feel sadness at leaving.

As I wrote to my mother, my mind teemed with unanswered questions: *What will she tell me about my father? My sisters and brothers?* Now that I was close to being reunited with my family, I almost dreaded what I might hear.

THIRTEEN
Crossing Over

The days of waiting for my mother's reply stretched out. Every day I watched for a letter. I kept going to the church, which gave me a used Bible. At the time, printing presses were not operating and Bibles were scarce. Over and over I read the verses that had encouraged and supported me in Siberia.

I was baptized June 1, 1947, and rededicated my life to the Lord. I could hardly wait to let my mother know. It was what my parents and Deacon Kuhn had wanted back then in my kitchen at home.

Finally a letter came from my mother in Schleswig (Holstein), telling of the family's joy in hearing from me and of their gratitude that their prayers had been answered. She wrote that my father was alive and all the family accounted for except Helmut, who was still a prisoner in Russia. And she sent me money to buy a ticket home. (I had worked without pay for my board and room.)

Unable to obtain a permanent visa, I made plans for a temporary visitation visa to visit my family, though I hadn't the slightest intention of returning. The man I worked for told me tickets were hard to get, so I should go to the station the night before and be first in line the next morning. They sold only so many tickets each day.

I sat alone wrapped up in my coat in the train station all night. The next morning twenty or more people stood in line. My overnight waiting paid off, for I soon pocketed my visitation visa and headed for the place where I worked.

The next day I packed a few belongings in a small bag and set off to catch the train in Berlin headed for the Russian border. I left with a tug of sadness, for the family where I worked had been very good to me, treating me like a daughter. We didn't say much by way of good-bye, but I think they knew I would not be back. I promised to write to them.

As I waited for the train, a tall woman dressed in plain dark clothes stood next to me. She began asking questions, and I felt open about talking to her.

"You want to cross over?" she asked softly.

"Yes," I replied. "My parents are in Schleswig."

"Well, it's not easy. Stay with me and we will go together. I've crossed many times."

"I have my ticket," I told her.

"There's more to it," she said—a comment which surprised me. "Stay with me," she repeated. She handed me a package of cigarettes and some black tea and said, "We may need that to bribe the guards."

When the train halted at the border, the woman peered out the window, then quickly drew back. "There's trouble here," she said. We could see Russian soldiers standing around the station. "This is as far as the train goes," the woman said. "We will go back one or two stations and see what it's like there."

As we rode back on the same train, I felt uneasy, wondering whether all my hopes of seeing my family would be dashed. But as I prayed, I felt reassured that God, who had helped me this far, would lead me safely to my parents.

At the first town back from the border, the woman signaled me to follow her off the train. We looked both ways. Not seeing anyone around, we set out on foot for the border. As we hiked across the open land and along a wooded section, I wondered where I would be if the Lord hadn't sent this woman to guide me across the border.

When we came to a fork in the road, the woman considered both paths, then chose what appeared to be the shortest way to the border. We hadn't walked far when a Russian soldier loomed out of the trees ahead of us. *Now what?* I thought. I couldn't bear to be turned back now. My new friend told me not to worry, and we walked right up to the Russian soldier. Silently I repeated the verse I had recited at my baptism: "Commit thy way unto the Lord; trust also in him; and he shall bring it to pass" (Psalm 37:5, KJV). I added, *Lord, I am trusting you.*

"Can you tell us the closest way to the border?" my companion asked the soldier. He must have been taken by surprise for he pointed the way. We gave him a package of cigarettes and walked as fast as we could without actually running. When we crossed the border, we jumped on a waiting truck already filled with people. A German driver ran the truck swiftly to the western train station. There we boarded a train for Hamburg and from there one to Schleswig.

As I turned to thank the woman who had been so helpful, she said quietly, "Tomorrow I go back again." Then she left me, and I never saw her again, this woman God used to direct my way across the border.

When the train pulled into Schleswig, my father and sister Ruth were waiting. Laughing and crying and hugging me, my father said, "Irma, Irma, God kept you safe. How we missed you."

"Yes," I whispered, choked with tears. "And I missed all of you, too." I wanted to stand there and talk, but Ruth poked me.

"Let's go," she said. "Mama's waiting." I couldn't hide my joy at seeing my father and sister again, and soon I would see my mother.

They took me to their tiny apartment, just a small room-and-a-half that my parents had made into a new home for all of us. My mother, with stooped back and hands crippled by arthritis, welcomed me through her tears, while my father led us in a prayer of thanksgiving.

"Irma," my mother cried, "we're so happy to have you here where all our family found each other."

"In this little place, Mama?" I looked around the small room.

"One by one. A good thing. Not many could stay here at a time. When Edeltraut was here, her children slept under the table." I laughed with the others. "Now you are safe," my mother said. "But we are still concerned about Helmut."

Questions and answers flew back and forth. "Siberia, Irma?" "You rode in a cattle train?"

"Ruth, did your baby live?"

"Only a few weeks. She was so tiny and sickly." So, Edeltraut's baby had died, too.

"Enough for now," my father said. "Let's have food. And sleep. It's getting late. Tomorrow we can talk again."

That night it took awhile for me to settle down to sleep. My mind kept churning over the amazing way God had protected our family and had brought us together again. *Although the war years have taken their toll from all of us, yet how rich we are,* I thought. *Even without money or possessions I have my family's love and God's love.*

That night in the little apartment I was filled with joy and peace and thanksgiving for his grace and mercy to me. He had brought me safely home!

FOURTEEN
Rebuilding Life

The following day my family and I talked and talked, laughing and crying together as we recounted some of our experiences. I learned that my mother and Ruth had fled East Prussia by boat and train soon after my capture. Finally arriving in Schleswig, they had found the tiny room-and-a-half apartment where our family would gather one after the other.

Ruth had given birth to her baby on a crowded Red Cross hospital train, with only my mother and a paramedic to assist her. Wounded soldiers lay in the bunks above and around her. Mother and Ruth had left our home in haste with only the clothes they wore and their purses. They had nothing for the baby until the Red Cross provided sheeting used for the soldiers' wounds.

My father had been conscripted into the Air Force and had later been captured by the Americans. He was released and arrived at the little flat in time for Christmas.

"He turned our sadness into joy just by knocking on the door," my mother said. "Laughing and hugging us, he asked if we had food. He thought I might be hungry so he saved his own meager rations and brought me bread." I could tell my mother was deeply touched by my father's concern for her, but it didn't surprise me, for my father had always been kind and considerate of others, especially those he loved.

My brother Kurt, who had been in the Air Force, had been captured by the Americans who sent him to a camp in Green Bay, Wisconsin. After his release he had crossed the ocean and had found his way home. He had located his wife and the two moved to Bavaria.

Next to come home was Ruth's husband. They had been living with my parents for some time under extremely crowded conditions. (Shortly after I returned, they found a room of their own and left. God knew my parents didn't have room for all of us in that tiny flat.)

Sadly, Edeltraut's husband was missing in action. Her very confused, aged mother-in-law had died. The baby Edeltraut had been expecting when I had been taken prisoner by the Russians, lived only a short time.

Edeltraut had returned to her farm near Mohrungen, hoping to raise enough food for her other children and herself.

When East Prussia was divided, the Poles occupied Mohrungen. One day the Polish government gave my sister an ultimatum: Either sign up and become a Polish citizen or get out.

"I'm a German citizen," Edeltraut had declared. After that response, the officers drove her out of her house with no time to make plans or even to collect clothing. With her children she fled, wearing only a homemade flannel slip. She finally arrived at my parents' little apartment a short time after Ruth's husband arrived.

When they learned Helmut's oldest boy lived in a foster home in Denmark, my parents made arrangements to care for him, adding one more to the family.

One day my father found out that Helmut was in a civilian prison camp in Russia. "Helmut's wife and other children were all killed on the boat by sharpshooters," he said sadly.

Because I had lived in crowded conditions for months in Russia, I could imagine how my family had slept on the floor and had tried to find enough food to eat. What had made it bearable here was our family's love for each other and for God.

Ruth laughed. "We had to eat in shifts. The children slept under the table. The church people helped Edeltraut find two rooms in the home of one church family. That eased the crowded situation here."

"Not knowing where you were, Irma," my mother said, "or if you were even alive was hard on us. We prayed and prayed for you and for Helmut, too."

"I could just feel it, Mama," I said softly. I related some of the times in Siberia when God had given me assurance that they had been praying for me, and how I had often experienced the providence of God, even so recently as when that unknown woman had helped me cross the border to freedom. Days and weeks slipped by before we had retold all our experiences.

I spared my parents the worst parts of my ordeal. They never inquired about such details. I was still a shy girl and would have been embarrassed to tell what I had suffered through no fault of my own. Probably the shock would have been too much for my mother. My parents never knew about the rapes, and only years later did I tell my sisters.

The first thing I did after finding my parents was to undergo a ten-day quarantine. Then I received a permanent pass and moved home.

The next step for me was to get a good physical checkup and see a dentist. The doctor gave me a good report—more evidence of God's care and protection. Without a toothbrush and nourishing food in Russia, I lost two teeth—which was better than I had expected.

We attended a nearby Baptist church where my father was an elder and sometimes filled in for the pastor. The children enjoyed Sunday school, and my sisters and I sang in the choir.

To prepare for a job, I took typing and shorthand in night school. Since jobs were scarce, I accepted the first one offered by the German placement office—that of housekeeper for a Norwegian family with three small children. I worked for my room and board and received a small payment, which I gave to my parents. Later I found that my father had saved the money to help buy a house for all of us.

I didn't know what the Norwegian family would be like, nor could I speak their language. Again God surprised me. The day after I moved in, the family held a weekly Bible study in their home for the servicemen. The husband, a captain in the Air Force, also served as chaplain.

With that family I learned to speak Norwegian well enough to answer the phone and care for the children. "Is it my wife speaking or is it Irma?" the husband would ask when I answered the phone. "You have picked up the language so fast," he said, "I can't tell you apart."

I also learned to reach out to others and to love people of all nationalities. Officers and their families frequently changed on the base, and I met many interesting people.

My father wanted to do something about our crowded living conditions. He began looking for a place he could rebuild for us now and for when he and my mother would be alone without us at home. My father and Kurt searched to find the right house. One day a letter came from Kurt:

> I've found the right house for you. It's in Hanau, close to Frankfurt, and the price is reasonable. Come over to see it. I think you will like it.

My father went to look at the house. "This big one?" he asked in dismay. I couldn't believe that Kurt would consider such a monstrosity. Before bombs had hit the house, it had had three stories, with high ceilings, brick walls, and a pitched roof.

My father shook his head. "All I wanted was a little house to rebuild." The building code at that time prohibited tearing down the remaining walls and building a small house in its place. The house had to be restored to its original size.

"Papa, you know how scarce houses are," Kurt said, pointing out the good qualities of the place. At last my father agreed it was the best we could do.

"Irma will have to go to work on it, too," my father said. Then he made arrangements to buy the house.

Although my father used to be a strong

man, the war had weakened him. I knew all about hard labor and had regained my strength. I gave up my job with the Norwegian family and moved to Hanau to help restore the house.

Before we hauled away great loads of rubble, we searched for every usable brick. Occasionally we found a pretty dish or a crystal vase that could be used. Most of the bricks had melted together in the fire, so I had to clean each one carefully so as not to break any. With very little money we prayed about each day's work. Now whenever my father received his pension, he would buy a sack of cement or other building material. I would mix cement in a large bucket and hand it up to him while he stood on a scaffold laying bricks.

Visitors dropped by and offered a little help. Kurt stopped on business trips and helped. Edeltraut lent a hand for a few weeks, but my father and I did most of the building alone. He asked other builders to stop by and give him estimates for doors and windows.

"Who do you have building for you?" the builders would ask. "The work looks good."

Papa would wink at me. "Well, the builders are my daughter and me." We laughed at the surprised looks on their faces.

As soon as we had restored the first floor, we fixed a little corner with walls and a roof so my mother could move in and do the cooking, thus saving the rent money on the little flat in Schleswig. My father set up a stove in another corner where the chimney stood, but no roof. When it rained, we took turns holding an umbrella over the stove while my mother cooked.

Nothing was easy those days. We worked long hours to enclose the first floor before winter. The most back-breaking job was laying three flights of terrazzo steps inside the house. Two people could hardly lift one stone step, but my father and I somehow managed. Many times I turned my head to keep my father from seeing my tears. He had developed a hernia, and I was afraid he would need surgery before we finished.

Rebuilding a house for us to live in was not our only task. We had to pick up the pieces of our lives, too, even as we watched the rebuilding of Germany.

Looking for work, I found a job typing and doing office duties in a nearby town and rode the bus back and forth. My hands were often sore and rough from handling the building bricks at night, making typing at the office more difficult.

By winter we had a roof, windows, and doors. In our spare time during the cold months we worked on the inside. When we finished, we had a comfortable house that was home to all of us for some years.

Gradually I came to understand that some of the brutal acts of the Russian soldiers had also been a part of Hitler's war crimes, that God has love and compassion for all people, and that God wants his followers to love their enemies. My Christian upbringing helped me deal with the past and gradually accept it. (As I write this book, I can honestly say I have no hate or hard feelings toward the Russians.)

The love and joy we had as a close and understanding family made life bearable. I would not trade all my experiences with anyone. They are mine to keep and learn from. I have found again and again that for those who trust in the Lord, he is always there when the need is greatest.

Young Irma on Easter 1934

Certificate of Release permitting Irma to leave Russia and make her way to Brandenburg (Berlin), dated September 26, 1946

Irma's Geburthaus (birthplace) in Thomareinen, now under Polish occupation

Papa on leave from the service in November 1944

The family watermill, taken in 1979

A happy family reunion in 1948

Mama and Papa standing on balcony of their rebuilt house

Irma and her first husband, Peter, and their two sons visiting Bavaria in 1963

Irma, a soldier who's weathered many storms, photo taken in 1980

Irma and John Stoll on their wedding day in 1977

EPILOGUE
Greater Dimensions

What happened to the young teenager who learned two of life's most important lessons—that we must place ourselves completely in God's hands and that he never abandons us? The reader must wonder what other events shaped her life. There are several.

MARRIAGE TO PETER AURICH

Peter and I met when my father and I were working to restore the house. After our marriage Peter talked constantly about the advantages of life in America and wanted us to move there. To leave my aging parents would be heart-wrenching. Still, I wanted to be where Peter could make a living for us, and we agreed it would be best to raise a family in Minneapolis.

In 1956 when our son Sieghard was five years old, we said good-bye to my parents and set out for the United States. I didn't know whether I would ever see my parents again. Our son Hans was born soon after we reached our new home.

Our sponsors, George and Jean Wahl, offered us an apartment in a building they owned, helped us get started, and took us to their Sunday school class called The Homebuilders, at First Baptist Church, Minneapolis. We were in good hands with those dear Christians and others at the church. Under Dr. Curtis B. Akenson's preaching, Peter became a Christian, and I grew spiritually.

We had come to the United States with little money and few possessions. Many times in the years following, we found our faith tested as we struggled with bad health and finances. Hans was ill as a baby; when he was two years old, he almost died because of convulsions. We faced big medical and hospital bills with no health insurance.

Still, we had a happy marriage and did things together as a family. We gave our boys basic Christian training and taught them the importance of commitment to God. We made sure they attended church and Sunday school with us.

Although Peter spoke English very well, it was a new language to me, and we spoke only German in our home. With the help of Sieghard and the media I picked up essential words. When Hans started school, the two languages confused him, so we decided to speak only English in our home.

THE SUICIDE

When my sons were much older, I entered a long black period when I suffered from crying spells and frayed nerves. It was because of Peter who had developed severe back pain, headaches, and finally depression. Doctors couldn't help him, and said he would have to learn to live with pain. Seeking to ease his misery, he took large doses of painkiller every day. The medicine altered his moods drastically, so much so that I began to fear for my life.

I believe Peter realized his condition. Perhaps because he didn't want to be a burden to us, he tried to end his life, first with carbon monoxide, then with an overdose of sleeping pills. Finally he succeeded, by hanging himself in his basement workshop.

Yes, there was sorrow and guilt, but also relief from a long and heavy strain.

I was again on my own—going to work, making decisions about selling our house, moving, raising a teen-ager. (By then Sieghard was married.) How I thank God I was not completely alone. Day by day his everlasting arms supported and guided me. Only a Christian knows that security.

To the best of my ability I had tried to follow my parents' example for my boys, praying for them daily and committing them to the Lord. Today both my sons love the Lord, are active in church, and lead balanced Christian lives.

THE RESTORATION

In 1977 I met psychologist Dr. John Stoll in the home of George and Jean Wahl, my longtime friends. About two months later, John surprised me by inviting me out for dinner. I, of course, accepted. We talked of many things—our children, single parenthood (we were each alone as parents), our mutual desire for God's will in our lives, and our willingness to serve him.

For a number of months we corresponded and saw each other from time to time. Without telling one another, each of us was praying for God's direction. When John asked me to marry him, I gladly accepted.

On a lovely warm day, October 22, 1977, we were married by Dr. Curtis B. Akenson in First Baptist Church, and I began a new period of my life—a truly happy one.

Today John is deeply involved in God's work as the executive director of ASK, a group of Christian businessmen who have joined "to offer people a relationship with Christ, and assist them in their Christian growth." He conducts Bible study classes, does professional counseling, and also finds time for writing.

As a psychologist my husband feels it is marvelous that my traumatic experiences of being captured, raped, starved, and imprisoned in Siberia have left no psychological scars, that I hold no grudges or anger and do not struggle with hang-ups.

How I thank God for carrying me in his arms of love during the war years and in prison camps. When I stumbled and fell, Christ's arms reached down to me again and again. His grace sustained me through all those experiences and strengthened me for the difficult times ahead.

I am reminded of the comforting words from Scripture:

> *Is your life full of difficulties and temptations? Then be happy, for when the way is rough, your patience has a chance to grow. So let it grow, and don't try to squirm out of your problems. For when your patience is finally in full bloom, then you will be ready for anything, strong in character, full and complete.* (James 1:2–4, TLB)

My parents are now gone to be with the Lord, but I am still grateful to them for having taught me spiritual truths, among them the need to trust in God, and for praying for me constantly.

I am thankful for all the experiences of the past, as they have helped me understand people in need. God has often used me to listen to the problems of others, especially over the phone, and I have been able to offer comfort and help.

For a long time I had felt a great desire to help the widows in my church. I knew what it was like to want to talk with someone who could understand.

Recently I started a monthly support group for widows in The Homebuilders class. Sometimes we do handicrafts or visit the local arboretum or go out for lunch. These women are also helped by sharing their problems with other widows.

Now my life holds many new experiences with even greater dimensions. Other than being a grandparent, I am happy to be John's constant companion in his ministries as together we serve the Lord.

More books from Greenlawn Press to build your faith!

Seven Steps Toward God
By Bill Beatty

Filled with practical wisdom, ***Seven Steps Toward God*** gives clear steps for accepting God's love and lordship and for living according to his plan. Beatty, an internationally known leader of the charismatic renewal, helps readers to pattern their lives after Jesus. He has included Scripture passages for reflection—making his book ideal for group instruction and retreats, as well as for personal use.
$4.50, paper, 102 pp.

**God Is at Work in You:
A Practical Guide to Growth in the Spirit**
By Ralph Rath

God Is at Work in You is perfect for anyone who has just come to know the Lord. Yet it also gives refreshing inspiration and counsel to any Christian wanting to grow in daily zeal for the Lord. Each chapter includes Scripture readings, real-life examples and discussion questions. Topics include praying daily, overcoming sin, discerning God's will and sharing the gospel with others.

"Would you like your Christian life to soar with the Spirit? Here's a book that will show you how."

—Bert Ghezzi, Contributing Editor, *New Covenant*
$4.95 paper, 92 pp.

Prayers for the New Evangelization
By Fr. Tom Forrest, C.Ss.R.

Here's an inspiring booklet of prayers and reflections to help readers talk to others more naturally and boldly about the Lord. Fr. Forrest is a gifted writer whose meditations foster a clearer vision of the Lord in daily life. This daily awareness of the Lord makes readers more willing and able to share the Good News with people every day.
$1.35, booklet, 32 pp.

Mighty in Spirit
By Joseph Bagiackas

Gives you an exciting modern look at the seven gifts of the Holy Spirit. Scripture passages, traditional wisdom and personal testimonies show how the gifts of the Spirit can enrich daily life. Written primarily—but not exclusively—for Catholic charismatics, this very popular book is in its fourth printing.
$2.45, booklet, 54 pp.

A Closer Look at the Enneagram
By Dorothy G. Ranaghan

Essential reading for proponents and opponents of the enneagram. This material is very helpful for pastoral ministers and spiritual directors. Dorothy Ranaghan shares the results of her extensive research into the background and teachings of the enneagram. Because of her findings, she cautions against use of the enneagram.
$3.95, booklet, 42 pp.

Continued on next page

The New Age: A Christian Critique
By Ralph Rath

Find out the facts! This handy and easy-to-read book contains a wealth of information to help readers identify the often subtle influences of the New Age in the world around them. Ralph Rath covered the New Age when it was still new for the *Oakland Tribune*. In this latest book he gives better understanding of the movement from Catholic and mainline Protestant perspectives.

"There's nothing comparable in terms of the amount of information in one source."
  —Fr. Emile Lafranz, lecturer: Christianity and the New Age

$8.95, paper, 347 pp.

Jesus Lives Today!
By Fr. Emiliano Tardif

Truly amazing and awe-inspiring stories of healings, life-changing wonders and conversions fill this personal testimony from a Canadian missionary to the Third World.

Starting with the story of a miraculous healing he himself received, Fr. Tardif builds people's faith as he humorously and joyously proclaims what God can do with those who open themselves to his power.

$6.95, paper, 152 pp.

The Imitation of Christ
By Thomas à Kempis. Translated by
Msgr. Ronald Knox and Michael Oakley

The most sought-after, most admired modern translation of the ***Imitation of Christ*** is available once again. For years, many people have treasured this particular translation for personal meditation and for meaningful gift-giving. Countless Christians have benefitted from reading this timeless classic. Everyone should have a copy of this wonderful translation to read over and over again—but especially during Lent.
$6.95, paper, 229 pp.

To Serve As Jesus Served
By Clem Walters

Ideal for prayer groups and adult-education programs, ***To Serve As Jesus Served*** is also suitable for personal use. This very popular book helps Christians serve with less frustration and more joy. Talk outlines, discussion questions and suggestions for practical application are included. The course has been tested and used for more than 10 years, benefitting thousands. Now in its third printing!
$3.95, paper, 132 pp.

Continued on next page

Order the books on the preceding pages today from your local Christian bookstore or directly from:

> Greenlawn Press
> Dept. E
> 107 S. Greenlawn Ave.
> South Bend, IN 46617

Payment must accompany order. Please add 6% for shipping and handling (**$1.50 minimum**). Payment may be by check, money order, VISA or Mastercard. If paying by credit card, please include your credit card number, your name as it appears on the card, the expiration date of your card, your phone number, and your signature on your order.

You can also order by phone using your VISA or Mastercard. Call 219-234-5088 between 8:30 AM and 4:30 PM EST, Monday through Friday. Please have your credit card ready when you call.